Soulful Words:

The Testimonies of Black Students' on the Manifestation of Institutional

Discrimination in Higher Education

By

Dr. CI

A Message

Dear Racism,

The disguise you don is elusive. We live in an era where your figment exists and no one believes in your existence. They say that the greatest trick the devil ever pulled off was making the world believe he did not exist. You have Houdinied the beneficiaries of White privilege and the enforcers of equality and meritocracy. You are indeed a magician, a chameleon, one who has historically evolved and hidden within our educational pipelines, political systems, and capitalistic society. You are indeed a master of disguise, forever mutating to formulize society's many constructs. The symbolic role of merit has revealed an irrational bias, one that lurks behind the modeling of White supremacy and privilege, and in some cases, Racially Stigmatized Identities in powerful positions. The fictitious lens of persistence, perseverance, and hard work ignite the flame of hateful speech, serving as justification for discrimination and mystifying the very notion of your existence. You have restrained multicultural knowledge and positioned the merely experiential as illegitimate, demoralized cultural norms with the intent of assimilation and adaptation, while in truth, you have used these to exterminate our cultural capital and community wealth.

The progression of social contextualization would suggest that your existence is a fabrication of those who fall victim to your wrath, those like me. A population of color, belittled at the hands of White supremacy, rendered invisible, has been engulfed by hatred founded on biological differences, rather than capability. Our humanity is clearly not forgotten, but it is overshadowed by misconceptions of meritocracy and the premise of equality, which seem obsolete. The fact that your political character is embedded deeply in the ideology of White supremacy which oppresses Racially Stigmatized Identities and manifests in multiple dimensions, has led to a continued struggle for our presence and civility.

I listened to your voice, the expressions that relegate me a useless, uneducated, lazy, and worthless being, deserving lashes of hate showered by the hands of your soldiers. You have numerous agents who do not recognize while victimizing others the ignorance that consumes your being. They have rejected our presence as we fight for the mere recognition of civility and humanity. In your time on this earth, you have enforced physical and mental genocide on my people, our worth, and progress. Just like you, WE, my people, are still here, and we will not disappear into thin air. Though you have a way of erasing our historical contributions, in your textbooks you condemn us to slavery, and you would have our children believe that we did not exist before slavery, WE will still remain here.

Because of your presence, I have examined your manifestation in the higher education system in one institution, though I recognize your existence in the pipelines of multitudes of higher education institutions. In this work, I offer, with heart and soul, the facts pertaining to your existence through the stories of nine participants, who narrated the presence you have maintained throughout their educational trials and tribulations. My only hope is that those who read this work will understand the communication and openness of these nine people. Through their testimonies they will show you nine perspectives, their experiences, and heartfelt expression of who they are and what they have faced and continue to face. They are familiar with the ways in which you operate, and their testimonies matter. Consider this work a message, an understanding of what is happening behind the walls of educational institutes. Our facilities are plagued with racial inequities and are in desperate need of reconstruction and transformation. Consider this an introduction and read carefully; the testimonies will articulate the feelings coming straight from their souls – they all have the right to be heard.

I am merely a representative of their stories, a messenger honored to bring to you these soulful words.

Sincerely,

Dr. Cheryl D. Ingram

An important note to the reader: Throughout this book I will be referring to the term *People of Color* (POC) as *Racially Stigmatized Identities* (Crocker, Major, & Steele, 1998; Goffman, 1963). This term refers to races that have been discriminated against through White supremacy. For more context, an identity that is stigmatized is socially devalued with negative stereotypes and beliefs attached to the identity (Crocker, Major, & Steele, 1998; Goffman, 1963). Moreover, stigma results in lowered power and status with resulting discriminatory outcomes (Link & Phelan, 2001).

Personal Acknowledgments

First and foremost I would like to thank the Universe. There were times when the practicing spiritual, emotional, physical, and mental wellness gave me strength to persevere through the physical and mental hurdles I stumbled on during this research. I would like to extend heartfelt gratitude to Bernice Ingram, my mother, and Tina Ingram, my sister – they instilled in me faith, motivation, compassion, and love. Faith steered me on during my academic and personal struggles. I could not have grown into the writer and scholar I am without the love and mentorship of my doctoral chair and advisor Dr. Rudolfo Chávez. Thank you for the patience, the teachings, respect, and discipline. *Sin su apoyo no estubiare aquí hoy, estaré siempre agradacida. Lo amo y le doy las gracias.*

To the rest of my doctoral committee, I want to extend my sincerest gratitude. Dr. Oesterrich you offered me insight about Black feminism for which I will forever remain thankful. Dr. Jeanette Haynes Writer was the first professor who taught me critical thinking. Dr. Cristobal Rodriguez introduced me to the process of conducting research at a doctoral level and gave me the opportunity to work as a graduate assistant.

I would like to take the time to thank the scholars of Bell hooks, Patricia Hill Collins, Tara Yosso, Daniel Solórzano, and Derrick Bell as well as other critical race theorists and Black feminists for their work. Your work and dedication helped forge the foundation for my research topic. I would also express my warm gratitude toward my

6

doctoral colleagues Leticia Burbano, Dr. Festus Addo Yobo, Dr. Ashley Ryan, Daniel Rubin, and Romina Pacheco for the inspiration and offered during this process. Further, I want to thank Dr. Linda Lacey for her mentorship and assistance throughout my graduate education. I would also like to thank my closest friends and family, too many to list, for the prayers, well wishes, and support through it all.

Last but not least, I want to thank every participant and every party that made this research possible. It was with your help, support, efforts, and actions that I had a foundation to build my scholarship on. Thank you!

Foreword

By Rudolfo Chávez Chávez, Emeritus

Regents Professor & Distinguished Achievement Professor

I first met Cheryl in a doctoral class. As the professor for the course, I was quickly drawn to her very human essences of excellence, courage, her powers of reflection, her unmitigated organic desire for hope, her clarity for knowing that we live in an interdependent reality and that we need one another, her strong commitment to service, her humility, her every growing imaginary and willingness to dream a liberatory vision centered on living a mission of freedom for all and a willingness to fight for it. I had rarely encountered such a human being much less worked with and learned from/with a doctoral student like Cheryl. She questioned with a fierce elegance and spoke boldly and bluntly about oppressive issues facing communities of Color. More importantly, she brought an elegance of intellectual curiosity rarely seen in the many doctoral students I had worked with. And, in my lingo of the day: Cheryl was not afraid to work, not afraid to read and reread, to sit down and deeply reflect on each word, each sentence, each paragraph, every chapter or article—to *study*. Then, once thoroughly prepared, Cheryl would share her ideas eloquently as well as challenge her classmates and me, her teacher, to think as deeply as she was striving to do. In this book, her acumen comes full circle with an unquenchable drive and unshakeable belief for a better day.

Dr. Cheryl Ingram's contribution is an inspiring voice that speaks truth to power. "Soulful Words: Testimonies of Black Students to the Manifestation of Institutional discrimination in the Academic and Social Structures of a Higher Education Institution" is testament to the insidious "manifests" of institutionalized, majoritarian macro and micro violence practiced with its oppressive and repressive tools of racism, sexism, and classism symbolically and systematically threaded and practiced in the everyday within the halls of the "ivory tower." Yet, with the overwhelming odds her research participants experienced, Dr. Cheryl Ingram was able to harvest the lived experiences expressed as participant testimonies who persisted and persevered to overcome with greater and lesser degrees the pernicious onslaughts of macro and micro aggressions embedded within the constructs of race, class, and gender as constructed within the halls of the ivory tower.

Notwithstanding, it cannot be left unsaid: the participants of this study could have been and (unfortunately) still could become victims of what is all too common when living in a nation that proports to have equality for its citizenry but where the majoritarian practices of white supremacy are the mainstay: the killings of George Floyd, Breonna Taylor, Atatiana Jefferson, Aura Rosser, Steven Clark, Botham Jean,

Philando Castille, Alton Sterling, Michelle Cusseaux, Freddie Gray, Fanisha

Fonville, Eric Garner, Akai Gurley, Gabriella Nevarez, Tamir Rice, Michael Brown,

Tanisha Anderson, and so many, many more. In the most tragic sense these souls are

the proverbial frogs in tepid water that soon boiled, tragically. Tragically, victims to

countless years of macro and micro violence when white supremacy goes

unchecked.

The participants of this study are, too, proverbial frogs in tepid water where the

metaphorical boiling ever-so-slowly could have made them in the image that a

society built on white supremacy would feel "comfortable" with. Cheryl focused her

study to a problem that needs to be constantly interrogated and that will illume

counter narratives of justice, love for one another and the other, and promote

personal and societal liberation for all. The testimonies within this study will

poignantly show what can be albeit a struggle—a struggle worth having. As John

Lewis so well captured: "Good trouble." With clear vision, Cheryl's research

illustrates a BlackCrit voice of scholarly substance and critical acumen. She asks a

simple question: How to determine academic and social trends of institutional

discrimination that influence the retention rate of Black students as they pierced

through the social and academic racial, gendered, and classed hierarchies of a

postsecondary educational institution?

In the throes of her doctoral work and more piercingly in her dissertation work, Dr. Ingram was exposed to what many other doctoral students would either have compromised their core values or succumbed to a lesser study simply to "get through" with palliatives of openness and lip-service to diversity. She was not deterred even when the institutional review body of Southwest University wanted to squelch her study or at least limit her research problem to a very narrow scope. This did not happen. After lots of back and forth, her study, as conceived was given the green light, she went to work. She began the interview process. She allowed herself two to three weeks between each interviewee. She reasoned that this was the best way to manage her time, to stay organized and focused, and to have the wherewithal to construct and organize the emerging themes daily evolving. She constantly reviewed the interviews, her notes, the Critical Race Theory and Black feminist literature, and journal writings of her participants. When in the thick of her study, she would come into our weekly meetings emotionally wrecked with tears in her eyes and a despondency that I was not used to seeing in Cheryl since, by nature, she was and is an uplifting entity of grace and joy.

Listening to the tragic stories of her participants, Cheryl came to an emotional and intellectual crossroad. Out of the ashes of personal and communal despair because of what she was uncovering, her alter-ego arose: Busara. Found in the classic critical race theory literature, it was inspired by Derrick Bell's "Geneva

Crenshaw" in his classic book *And We Are Not Saved* (1987) and Richard Delgado's "Rodrigo Crenshaw" from *The Rodrigo Chronicles* (1995). Bell and Delgado created their alter egos to reinforce and bring themselves to understanding complex phenomena but more importantly to create a human voice to the theoretical frameworks of CRT so as to engage in critical discussions of race and racism in education.

Sometimes out of nowhere, Busara appears with a wisdom that only comes through struggle, through pain and anguish, through living with joy and, yes, living through tragedy. Busara (Swahili translation for wisdom) represents, in full force, an alternative narrative in the tradition of Black Feminist and Critical Race Scholarship and other literary works. Busara is a symbolic representation of Cheryl's subconscious. Busara appears only to engage in critical dialogue with Cheryl during times of her confusion, to reiterate and reaffirm the why of her study. The engagement is refreshing. Speaking parts include the participants' dialogue with one another and with Cheryl, as well as Cheryl's insights quilted by her field notes and journal entries. Her field notes and interviews became the substance to bring the storied lives of her participants that emerged to create a counter story that informs, surprises, and assists the reader to rethink her or his assumptions about race, about the notion of equality when educating the Other, and about how white supremacy is insidiously entangled within the very core of what is a higher education for Black

12

students and I dare to say for most if not all students of color as well as white students.

The courage to understand our future as well as act on it will be only as great as our desire to understand our present-past in light of the tragic happenings that have become central to our lives: social, economic, racial, and LGBTQ violence that has unfolded to a great extent with or without our collective actions; for all practical purposes there is no neutrality on a moving train—this metaphorical train has left the station by the collective and individual choices a collective and diverse populace on board has made. Recent events brought on by the killing of Mr. George Floyd is evidence of this. The collective choices to think, value, and act with commitment and responsibility will inform how our collective futures transpire. It is with this imperative that our collective and individual identities are transformed within ourselves and with the Other as we position our lives to live with an awakening to civic responsibility whilst living a social and economic justice in a society that is diverse with a still-in-becoming democratic underpinnings. This book addresses the many difficult and humbling lessons that Dr. Cheryl Ingram learned in this work of love and transformation as a first-person witness in her journey coupled with her courageous participants whose painful experiences were transformed into beacons of light that will guide and embrace a society that practices equity and justice for all.

Dedication

This dissertation is dedicated to the following:

Bernice Ingram

November 1, 1950-January 08, 2015.

My Best Friend

Erika Denise Williams

July 12, 1981–February 19, 2008

Calvin Lynn Cotton

June 6, 1996–June 29, 2012

Corey Paul

1978–August 18, 2008

and

Jacque Stanton

May 31, 1987–December 2012

Larry D. Johnson Jr.

March 20, 1983-August 16, 2020

Gone too soon but never forgotten.

Abstract

This work was informed by the theoretical frameworks of Black feminism and Critical Race Theory (CRT). The aim was to determine the academic and social trends of institutional discrimination that influence the retention rate of Black students as they traverse through the social and academic hierarchies of a post-secondary educational institution (Collins, 1998; Collins, 1998; Tate, 2006). The qualitative method of case study was used to investigate the phenomenon (Yin, 1994, 2003). The study was conducted in a four-year public Hispanic serving institution in the southwest region. The participants were grouped into three collective cases: push-outs, college graduates, and currently enrolled students, which allowed organic themes to emerge. The methods used to collect for crystallization of the data analysis were observation, journaling, field notes, and historical document analysis. The data were reported in the form of testimonies and a counter story (Solórzano & Delgado Bernal, 2001; Solórzano & Yosso, 2000, 2001, 2002) to emphasize the institutional discrimination that participants experienced and counter the prevalent, majoritarian narrative of diversity documented by virtual and actual archival data by the College of the Southwest. The findings showed institutionalized racism, symbolic violence, and the persistence and perseverance of participants. Recommendations include the development of diverse institutional practices and student advocacy. Lastly, a first-person epilogue that touches upon the

15

process of transformation of the researcher throughout this study offers the researcher's

perspective for a new beginning.

Contents

Chapter 1

Introduction to Research Study

Introduction

Black students' enrollment to post-secondary educational institutions has been

consistently below the national average (National Center for Educational Statistics

[NCES], 1983, 1990, 2000, 2010). Black students only account for 5.8% of the total

enrollment in both public and private four-year post-secondary institutions in the United

States. White Anglo-Americans account for 62.3% while Hispanics comprise 4.3% of

the total enrollment in post-secondary educational institutions, both public and private

(Knapp et al., 2010). Black people have one of the lowest enrollment and graduation

rates in four-year post-secondary educational institutions as well, specifically while

attending traditionally White institutions. A study of students who graduated with a

bachelor's degree or its equivalent within six years conducted by the NCES (2010)

confirmed that approximately 67% of Asians/Pacific Islanders, as compared to 60%

Whites, 48 % Hispanics, 42% Blacks, and 40% American Indians/Alaska Natives,

completed their program of study within the stipulated timeframe. This pattern held for

Asians/Pacific Islanders, Whites, and Hispanics at each institution type while Blacks and

American Indians/Alaska Natives consistently had the lowest graduation rates among

the five racial/ethnic groups (NCES, 2010).

21

In 2010, African Americans accounted for 12.6% of the American population. In this group, 31.5% Black families live either at or below the poverty line. Living below the poverty line is described as a family of four living either at or below a yearly income of $15,000. Black people account for 24.7 % of total Americans living below the poverty line. Living at the poverty line signifies a family of four living off a yearly income estimated in the range of $15,000–$24,000. The NCES (2010) showed that Black children living with both married parents account for 18% of children living with families in poverty, though within the Black population living with children, married families only account for 34%. Data indicated that 49% of Black children live in poverty with single Black mothers while another 28% live in poverty with single Black fathers. Single Black fathers account for only 6% of the total Black population living with one or more children. The educational attainment of Blacks is still rising despite economic hardships, yet the rate of incompletion within these institutions remains consistently high (NCES, 2011; Journal of Blacks in Higher Education [JBHE], 2012).

The Census Bureau (2011) also reported that in 2008, only 12.8 % of Black people earned a college/professional degree from a post-secondary institution. The NCES (2012) reported that between 1980 and 2011, the secondary education rate of Black students increased from 77% to 88% and the completion gap within secondary institutions between Blacks and Whites narrowed. The same data also revealed that in post-secondary educational institutions, the completion gap for bachelor's degree between Blacks and Whites has increased. However, the gap in attainment of a master's degree between the two groups does not show a significant difference. The United States Census Bureau (2011) reported that, in 2009, the national unemployment rate was 9.3%. The Black population at the same time accounted for 14.8% of the unemployed, while the White population accounted for 8.5% even though they represent 72.4% of the US population. Therefore, there is a clear overrepresentation of the Black population in terms of unemployment and poverty in this country.

In 2008, Census data also showed that people who earn a bachelor's degree earn $20,000 more annually than those with only a high school diploma, ranging from $30,000–$40,000 less than workers with a graduate degree (Census Bureau, 2000, 2010, 2011). The completion of college is beneficial to one's quality of life and economic standing and should not go unnoticed and uninvestigated. Research data have demonstrated that educational completion above a high school degree is an important contributor to economic and social success (Census Bureau, 2000, 2010). The United States Department of Labor (2012) reported that a massive number of job layoffs happened between 2007–2012 in industries that did not require their workers to hold post-secondary educational degrees. During this period, the unemployment rates for Blacks increased to the highest percentage they have been in decades. Over two decades later and during a time of economic recession, Black people accounted for the largest group of unemployed workers at 14.4% (US Census Bureau, 2000, 2010). The less likely a worker is to hold a post-secondary educational degree, the lower is the likelihood of them maintaining stable job positions. The United States Equal Employment Opportunity Commission (EEO, 1974) stated that people who faced de facto discrimination in the past suffered more layoffs during economic recessions as they occupied a lesser number of senior positions in the job market (Feagin & Sikes, 1980). In 2011, the EEO reported that color-based charges consistently increased between 1997–2011 as more Racially Stigmatized Identities reported race-based layoffs and other forms of discrimination and were awarded monetary settlements. The EEO also reported that in 2011, Black laborers represented only 3% of senior level management positions, 7% of mid- and first-level positions, comprising 23% of service workers, 16.4% of office and clerical workers while only representing 13.6% of the total workforce in the private sector (EEO, 2011). The requirements for senior-, mid-, and first-level positions in the job market are highly dependent on the level of education of the applicants. These economic statistics reflect the unemployment numbers of Black people and their relation to educational practices; this also indicated the group's social and economic position in the United States. Disadvantages in the job market are based on educational privileges accorded by educational institutions and their practices (Feagin & Sikes, 1980; Klein, 2011; Norton, 2011; Saltzburg, 2011).

The economic and social conditions of Blacks in this country demand an assessment of the historical and current educational conditions created by the political, cultural, and financial privileges associated with the completion of a bachelor's degree. That considered, the overall number of students who received a bachelor's degree within the past decade has almost doubled, while the number of post-secondary degrees achieved by Black students in post-secondary educational institutions remains at a standstill (U. S. Department of Education, 2000, 2011). In 2011, the U. S. Department of Education reported that the gap between Blacks and Whites with a bachelor's degree widened by almost 6%. The same report stated that 44% of Black children in elementary school and 18% Black children in high school attend high-poverty educational institutions compared to 6% White children in elementary school and 2% in high school.

The Problem and Purpose of the Study

Research showed that the enrollment of Black students in post-secondary educational institutions demonstrated various instances of both enrollment and decline rates throughout the last 19 years (Allen, 1992; IRPOA, 2010; NCES, 2011; Wilds & Wilson, 1998). Though the enrollment rate for Black students has varied in numbers, the low percentages in graduation and retention rates have remained consistent. Black students attend educational institutions where they face racial microaggressions, hostile racial climates, under-resourced programs and lack the mentoring and institutional practices needed to promote educational success (Davis, 1994; Feagin & Sikes, 1995; Lynch, 2002; Solórzano, 2000). According to Allen (1992) and Frueda-Kwarteng (2005), there is consistent historical and current data regarding retention and

25

discrimination issues of Black students in mentoring and post-secondary institutions. The aforementioned studies of Astin (1968), Feagin and Eckberg (1995), Frueda-Kwarteng (2005), Kursch (2006), and Lynch (2002) provide data on racial dynamics, mentoring, and issues of powerlessness that negatively affect the retention and enrollment rates of Black students in post-secondary institutions. Notwithstanding, studies also indicate that a number of Black students indeed complete their degree programs in post-secondary educational institutions (NCES, 2010, 2011). However, one aspect goes unnoticed within these studies, the incorporation of alternative perspectives within the data. Previous studies conducted by Feagin and Eckberg (1995), and a decade later Frueda-Kwarteng (2005), produce important data that engages the impact of racial microaggressions, blatant racism and prejudice, and other discriminatory practices Black students face within post-secondary institutions. One important critical question missing in this literature is: after all of the administrative discriminatory practices have been evaluated, what is the counter story?

This purpose of this study is to examine the testimonies of Black students by investigating their academic and social collegiate experiences, concluded by the analysis of the intersections of race and education (Graham, 2000; Weiner, 2003). This study analyzes multiple student perspectives regarding the social and academic practices that affect Black students' undergraduate/graduate enrollment, as well as their experiences with the administrative practices, campus activities, and campus staff and faculty in the institution. The study is unique because it critically investigates the perspectives of three categories of Black college students: the push-out, the currently enrolled, and the graduates of post-secondary institutions. The aspect researchers must continuously probe is how the American higher educational system supports the manifestation of and perpetuates racial and discriminatory practices through administrative academic and social procedures. Historically, Blacks have represented large numbers of secondary and post-secondary educational incompletion rates, unemployment rates, and comprised a large proportion of Americans below or at the poverty line. The statistics of poverty among Black people in the United States is systematically repetitive. Education within the United States is political, reflective of the mainstream elite White culture that devalues and excludes Racially Stigmatized Identities and the importance of their cultural, historical, economic, and social contributions (Apple, 1985, 2000; Bell, 1992; Giroux, 2004; Pinar, 1989, 2003, 2005).

Research also indicates that close to 50% of Blacks who enroll in public institutions in the U.S. do not complete their four-year degree programs and that the enrollment of Black students in post-secondary educational institutions has declined throughout the last 19 years (Allen, 1992; IRPOA, 2010; U. S. Department of Education, 2011; Wilds & Wilson, 1998). It is further noted that minority students, particularly Black students, drop out at higher levels than their White counterparts in post-secondary educational institutions (NCES, 1990, 2000, 2010; Roscigno, 1999).

27

Similar to Feagin (2000) and other researchers, I contend that racism is manifested in the social rhythms of everyday life in the United States, especially within our educational institutions, and such practices influence the retention rate of students of color (Delgado & Stefanic, 2001; Collins, 2004). The completion of educational degree programs impacts the economic, political, and social conditions of this student group.

This study relies on previous research. As the primary researcher, I engage in multiple dialogues with Black students; the research, in effect, entails Black students narrating their counter story. The problem does not lie in the enrollment of Black students in post-secondary educational institutions, it rather lies in the dynamics that affect the retention rate of these students such as racial microaggressions, lack of faculty representation, and multiple institutional forms of discrimination.

Discriminatory Practices Diagnosed by Theoretical Frameworks

This study adopts the theoretical frameworks of Black feminism and CRT. These theories uncover the situational impact that academic and social hierarchies, such as administrative practices within institutions, have on the intersections of race and education throughout the educational trajectory of Black students (Collins, 1998; Collins, 1998; Tate, 2006). Although race remains at the forefront, the theoretical frameworks are open to other intersectional discriminations that may surface during the research practice. This investigation examines the power of institutional policies, in addition to allowing the critical examination of administrative, social, and academic procedures that evaluate their institutional manifestations in the everyday college life of

Black students. The theoretical frameworks will provide a foundation that should assist

in further understanding the dynamics that lead Black students to coercive discharge,

known as the pushout,[1] as well as retention (Allen, 1992; Feagin & Sikes, 1995; Fine,

1991; Matsuda et al., 1993).

Enrollment trends of Racially Stigmatized Identities have altered over the past

three decades in post-secondary educational institutions; overtime, students of color

have enrolled in multiple post-secondary educational institutions (NCES, 1990, 2000,

2010). When focusing on the educational status of a marginalized group, one must

attempt a critical evaluation of the economic and social conditions of such populations.

Such systematic placements are proven to directly and indirectly impact dynamics

through race and class (Collins & Anderson, 2001; Marable, 2006; Yosso, 2005, 2009).

The completion of education at post-secondary and secondary levels contributes to an

improvement of economic and social conditions of marginalized and oppressed groups.

In part, this research critically investigates the circumstances Black students endure in

predominantly White colleges and universities, which could be a manifestation of the

malpractices of power that perpetuate institutionalized discriminatory practices

(Sólorzano et al., 2000; Valencia, 2010). Power in this context is defined by Patricia Hill

---

[1] Pushout was a term used by Michelle Fine in 1991, to describe students who are forced to leave educational institutions due to unresponsive institutional arrangements.

Collins (2000) as mediated action by dominant forces to engage in discriminatory practices on the basis of race through forced political and non-political marginalizations oppressing students of color, in particular Black students (Crenshaw, 2002). This definition of power by Collins assisted in contextualizing the following phenomenon in the research investigation: the effects of institutional policies and procedures on the retention rates of Black students in post-secondary educational institutions.

To analyze such implications, one must explore multiple theoretical perspectives that not only identify impact but also the political positions that perpetuate policies and procedures within the institution itself, placing such structures in the position of power and Black students in a spot of oppression. This study proposes to critically evaluate social and academic instances of institutional practices that impact the retention and graduation of Black students within post-secondary settings.

Rationale, Significance and Theoretical Framework of the Study

The Importance of the Counter Story vs. the Majoritarian Story Informing Educational Research

Post-secondary institutions are public social, political, and cultural institutions that influence and miseducate through the knowledge they impart and the power they exercise through policies and classroom practices for all student populations, whether Black or not (Crenshaw, 2002; Dixson & Dingus, 2007; Gildersleeve et al., 2011; Villalpando, 2004). The experiences of Blacks in the educational system have been narrated through a White, racist, privileged perspective, known as the "majoritarian story" (Montecinos, 1995; Sólorzano & Yosso, 2002). The refusal to acknowledge the existence of White privilege in our education system, especially in higher education, perpetuates racism and overshadows the experiential perspective that defines the educational journeys of Racially Stigmatized Identities (Crenshaw et al., 1995). Critical race theory and Black feminist theory offer the theoretical lens to understand the multi-dimensional perspectives of institutional practices. One perspective investigated within this study involves the direct and indirect impacts of the phenomenon of Black students' pushout rate in higher education. The testimonies of Black students attending post-secondary institutions were collected. Their stories contextualized and explained issues and experiences that influenced decisions to remain with an institution, the pushing and/or dropping out of these students and the several approaches they used as survival tactics in the face of institutionalized discrimination.

The realities of high urban poverty rates and economic inequities that manifest within the marginalization and oppression of communities of color and Blacks in particular have created a need for a reconstruction as well as the reinterpretation of the aim of higher education policies and practices in order to address the need for social and academic improvement (Anyon, 2005; Hernandez & Raymond, 2002; Sleeter, 2005). These practices must be evaluated through qualitative research practices which employ testimony and legitimize experiential knowledge through the counter story.

Borrowed from CRT, the counter story refutes the majoritarian narrative and acceptance of the dominant culture's interpretation of the "accepted" way of political practices in post-secondary educational institutions, which constitute the majoritarian story (Solórzano & Yosso, 2002). Typically, in the institutional context, there is an absence of a counter story, a silence created by the dominance of the majoritarian/stock story where White privilege manifests itself. Therefore, this absence demands an alternative narrative, one that recognizes the importance of voices from the marginalized and oppressed, populations that endure realities unique to subordinated groups, such as the people of color.

Testimonies provide a language to bridge gaps in imagination and conception that can create differences (Delgado & Stefanic, 2001; Weiner, 2003). Bauman (2004) argued about the importance of including storytelling:

> Stories aid the seekers of comprehension by separating the relevant from the irrelevant, actions from their settings, the plot from the background, and the heroes or the villains at the centre of the plot from the host of supernumeraries and dummies (p. 17).

Research has demonstrated that students dropping out is a clear indication that society as a whole and educational institutions in particular are not providing the welfare of all its student citizenry (Chávez et al., 1991; Journal of Blacks in Higher Education, 2000; Lynch, 2002; Sólorzano et al., 2009). While Chávez et al.'s study showed the lack

32

of cultural inclusion in post-secondary education institutions, it still refers to students of color from a dropout perspective. Inclusive practices with regard to student ethnicities, cultures, and life experiences have to be adopted as a component of higher education not just in terms of curriculum but also administration, academics, and the social aspect (Hooks, 1994; Freire, 1996); this is essential to the success rate of all students. This study relied on frameworks and tenets of Black feminist theory and critical race theory to explore the educational institution as a system of oppression for Black students (Collins, 2000; Solórzano et al., 2000). As a theoretical framework, Black feminist theory speaks to and addresses resistance mechanisms used by Black students in institutions that discriminate against them on the basis of race in education (Andersen & Collins, 2004). Critical race theory confronts the racial climate that Black students experience in college campuses and the direct and unconscious racism prevalent in the everyday lives of these students (Solórzano et al., 2000; Davis, 1994).

Critical race theory and Black feminism challenge the dominant ideology of objectivity, meritocracy, race neutrality, and equal treatment and color-blindness in our educational institutions perpetuated through mainstream knowledges (Parker, 1998). These two theoretical frameworks include a theoretical treatment of multiple forms and means of discrimination such as race and education. The absence of care and equitable opportunities of access and treatment of Racially Stigmatized Identities in post-secondary educational institutions due to interest convergence, the subtle underlying agenda, is critically investigated throughout this study. This study explored institutional

political and pedagogical procedures through Black students' perspectives which placed

post-secondary institutions in positions of power. The administrative, social, and

academic practices within this marginality were explored through a qualitative research

methodology, the political discourse of the research participants, in addressing the topics

of educational outcomes and race. The discourse evaluating institutional practices in

higher education encompassing White privilege and the manifestation of discrimination

at the intersection of race and education must also allow confrontational research

practices and their ability to impact means of equity, equality, and justice (Brah &

Phoenix, 2009; Hooks, 1984).

The focus of my research was not simply an investigation into the academic and

social discourses, which included an analysis of the impact of college administration,

staff, peers, and faculty in the educational trajectory of Black students (Olsen & George,

2004). The analysis included but was not limited to experiences within the educational

trajectory of Black students in four particular areas: faculty, administrative, peer to peer,

and staff interactions within the institution. The evaluation of classroom practices in this

study looked at the attitudes of classroom professors and the participants' opinion on

whether or not they feel these educators incorporate or discriminate against their cultural

capital. My study also investigated participant testimonies regarding the inequities and

injustices that emerge between Black students and multiple entities that might be

34

consciously or unconsciously discriminating against Black students in everyday institutional practices. Regardless of whether the discriminatory action was conscious or unconscious, the analysis proved that institutionalized discrimination was extremely prominent.

Research Questions

The research questions were broken down into three categories to examine the three different populations within the research study. The primary focus of the study is stated in the following research question:

1. What academic[2] and social experiences do Black students have in post-secondary educational institutions that impact their graduation with a bachelor's degree?

Sub Questions

2. What were Black students' social and academic experiences with the university's administration that they believe impacted their post-secondary educational experience?

---

[2] Shelia Slaughter and Larry Leslie in *Expanding and Elaborating the Concept of Academic Capitalism* (2001) use the term "academic" refer to the way in which post-secondary educational institutions create market-like behaviors to regulate educational policy in post-secondary educational institutions. The political context involves formal educational procedures and means of scholarship that build foundations of learning by academics who educate and form policies within these institutions.

3. What were Black students' experiences regarding the curriculum[3] in university courses that represent academic contexts which impacted their presence in those academic contexts?

4. What were Black students' experiences regarding academic and social support systems present or absent in the university and how are such systems important influences on their degree program completion?

Impact Question

5. How can multiple experiences of Black students in post-secondary educational institutions transform institutional policies and procedures to help improve their graduation rates?

Positionality of the Researcher

I am a Black female who has experienced institutionalized discrimination first hand, and I am interested in the perspective of other students who may be facing the same trials and tribulations – this constitutes my privilege. My position as the researcher is to adequately and accurately relay the participant testimonies to students and make them beneficial for them in their everyday lives and experiences in the educational institution in an objective manner. The positioning relative to the participants is

---

[3] William Pinar's (2005) What is Curriculum Theory and Michael Apple and Landon Beyer's (1998) The Curriculum: Problems, Politics, and Possibilities define the educational state of curriculum as a political discourse dominated by a White elitist, right-winged, standardized model. This model permits a dominant political control of the accessibility of information in education, what teachers should teach, and what information students in the public school educational system should gain.

subjective, since in research it is impossible for a researcher to maintain absolute objectivity, especially when the research topic is something they are passionately attached to and it stems from personal experience. In my research, my status positions my privilege. When conflicts within a position are admitted and are allowed openly, they are more manageable and likely to be evolved into research tools (Marshall & Rossman, 2011; Copp, 2008). The purpose of inviting a second opinion from an outside party not involved in the study was that they could analyze my position if and when it created potential blinders for my research. At the beginning of this study, I had to rethink my current position on campus and my possible contributions to a community facing multiple forms of discrimination.

A major realization for me has been that I have needed to reflect and critically analyze my position growing up as a poor Black female and the way in which the knowledge I gained outside of mainstream knowledge within my own community was rich in nature and positively influenced my research. I had to repeatedly ask the questions: "How did I get here?" and "why did I stay here in this institution" in light of the memories that surfaced in the qualitative historical analysis phase of the research. My interpersonal dilemmas created a sense of excitement and passion for my research topic that kept me motivated and focused. The theoretical frameworks of Black feminism and critical race theory supported my subjective stance on the topic and academic grounding. Black feminism addressed the oppressions of racism, sexism, and classism practiced by White, elitist, male-dominated institutions such as the one I investigated. Black feminism explained the exploitation of the experiential knowledge of the Black woman, the maliciousness of hegemonic higher educational structures to exclude her presence, and how these issues continue to exist when a grounded and thorough perspective is assumed (Hooks, 1981; Collins, 2000; Collins, 2004).

I thought that if I wanted to make an impact and demonstrate the significance of my work, I needed to find a balance between my privilege and oppressions in order to remain ethical. I also wrote my field notes, to ensure I reflected on issues of ethics, mistakes, and used accurate data collection methods, and this facilitated the process of self-reflection within my research.

Conclusion

The aim of the first chapter was to provide a clear and in-depth overview of my study. I attempted to provide a rationale and purpose for the study while offering the reader a brief insight into the objective of my research. The background provided in this chapter is meant to inform the reader about the historical and present data that forms the genesis of the research while also offering a transition into the problem statement of the study. I wanted to offer a peek into my perspective as a researcher; therefore, I included the theoretical frameworks that will serve as a foundation for the study to create meaning and a critical lens into the diversity of Black students and their experiences in post-secondary educational institutions through their testimonies.

Chapter II

Literature Review

Chapter Summary

The literature reviewed within this section focuses on the power and authority of educational structures in relation to the experiences of Black students in higher education. The examination of key concepts throughout scholarly discourses has been addressed through theoretical frameworks that identify multiple dynamics and their relation to Black students in higher education institutions.

Analyzing Race and Education: A Critical Race Theory and Black Feminist Perspective

Research conducted by Black feminists such as Hooks (1994) and Collins (2000) highlight an absence of cultural understanding that leads to culture becoming irrelevant between educational institutions dominated by White elitist and capitalistic administrations and the non-White privileged populations that attend these institutions. This lack has created a hostile and inadequate learning environment, for Black students in particular attending such educational institutions, by enforcing a sense of powerlessness and systematic discriminatory practices in their educational pursuit (Fredua-Kwarteng, 2006; Smith et al., 2009). According to the work of leading scholars, racial microaggressions are a contributing factor in the poor completion rate of students of color (Solórzano et al., 2000; Swim et al., 2003). The studies mentioned highlighted

40

racial microaggressions that Black students face on college campuses from their White counterparts. The research of these theorists indicate institutionalized oppressions that Black students face due to the social constructs of race, class, and gender at the hands of the dominant White privileged ideologies.

The research works mentioned established the foundation to categorize and investigate institutionalized discriminatory practices and cultural politics by naming oppressive higher education institutions. Hooks (1994) discusses educational institutions that were and continue to be dominated by White privileged ideologies where students are taught obedience and knowledge is centered around information only; the practice of freedom for Black students has been eliminated within these institutions. Studies that embrace the theoretical frameworks of Black feminism and critical race theory present discourses that address marginal impacts within institutions and the intersectional patterns of race and class by their ability to shape multiple political dimensions within such systems (Brah, 1996, 2000; Crenshaw, 2009). The studies of Brah (1996) and Crenshaw 92009) consistently illustrate marginalization, isolation, and other forms of subordination that lead to oppression in the educational experience of the Black student population. Historically, critical race theory and Black feminism have analyzed the way in which the political policy of whiteness institutionally affects and impacts intersections of race, class, and gender (Bell, 1987, 1992; Crenshaw et al., 1995; Gillborn, 2009; Marvin & Lynn, 2009; Tate, 1995). The importance of the theoretical strengths of critical race theory and Black feminist studies stem from their ability to place race at the forefront of other intersections, without undermining their importance. A process that educational positions must adopt is raising and evolving critical consciousness. During the transformational process, educators, leaders, and researchers must surmount and then confront an internal organic resistance. Scholars who discuss resistance require that in order to subjectively critique and analyze the politics involved in intersectional discrimination, especially within policy formation, teachers and learners must be willing to admit their own biases, cultural or racial (Sleeter, 2001; Yosso, 2005). Critical race theory and Black feminism both dictate a need to place the conditions of Blacks in the United States into a historical context, especially in educational institutions, because that allows the space to analyze the impact of political policy and structures on race.

Black feminism and critical race theory analyze the subtleness of racism in educational practices and the ability of racial structures to oppress Racially Stigmatized Identities (Collins, 2004; Crenshaw, 2009; Delgado & Stefanic, 2001; Matsuda et al., 1993). The context within Collins (2004) and Crenshaw (2009) distinguishes the impact of intersectional discrimination and how they impact the everyday lives of those physically and sociologically oppressed. For instance, if one believes that education is the key to success, then the impact of poverty and the privilege of wealth must be considered as well: classism is an issue (Apple, 1996; Mickelson & Smith, 2004; Pinar

2005). The issue is substantiation within the regulation of cultural marginality of people of color, especially in the institutional priorities of post-secondary education that promotes a technological and scientific societal progression which is market-driven within a capitalist framework – this must be continuously evaluated (Apple, 1996; Mickelson & Smith, 2004; Pinar 2005). Statements formulated on the premise of democracy that emphasize so-called equality meted out by education do not consider the capitalist practices within our society that overlook the well-being of the marginalized and politically, socially, and economic oppressed groups. BlackCrits and LatCrits use their research paradigms to analyze race as a social construction, in particular biological factors and how these social constructions influence curriculum and policy-making in educational institutions (Bell, 1992; Delgado, 1995; Delgado & Stefanic, 2001; Ladson-Billings & Tate, 1995; Smith-Maddox & Solórzano, 2002).

BlackCrits and LatCrits dissect the construction of legal statues of race and the way in which race impacts the systematic structures in education. The objective construction of race directly creates systematic penalties and discriminatory actions directed towards people of color. Matsuda et al. (1993) and Cornell and Murphy's (2002) works reinforce the negative impacts of racism in our society and the way it has become commonplace due to the frequency of its manifestation. The devastation experienced by victims of normalized racist actions, offenses, and acts that are verbally and physically violent in nature is negated due to the underemphasis on racism and its

43

relation to the educational and overall living success rate of people of color. Solórzano and Yosso (2002) and Tate (2008) discuss the social arrangement of society that often leads to the rationalization of racial bias overshadowed in our institutions with the misperception of "equal opportunity for all". Paulo Freire (1970, 1973) recognized the absence of neutrality in education, stating that all educational institutions are political. He recognized that education is built on the premise of political purpose and that we as a society must become conscious of this malpractice to kickstart a cycle of change. Through his writings, Freire (1970) asserted that the purpose of schools is to promote the status quo, and educators must become cultural workers, empowering students through transformational approaches to protect their cultural being (Freire, 1998). Black students, especially those attending predominantly White institutions that enforce meritocratic ideologies of elitism which reflect a White, male, Eurocentric American society, are more likely to be rendered invisible within the higher educational system. To address this invisibility, the use of counter story becomes central to understanding the phenomenon by cross analyzing race and its impact on education through the experiential testimonies of Black students in this study, through the lenses of critical race theory and Black feminist theoretical frameworks.

The Discriminatory Act of Racial Subordination in the Consciousness of Education

Bell (1992) and Delgado and Stefanic (2001) outlined the discriminatory act of racism and why such subordination has become an internal and external organic process.

44

Critical race theory scholars argue that the internalized socializations of racism, sexism, classism, and other acts of subordination have become assimilated into our everyday thought processes and accepted as natural requirements throughout the field of education as well as multiple disciplines in higher education. DeCuir and Dixson (2004) delved into the permanence of racism and its governance in educational domains and how acts of racism perpetuate the acceptance of privilege within our educational institutions. Thus, Racially Stigmatized Identities become participants in their own dehumanization, a practice born out of the construction of an oppressive capitalist system (Fischman et al., 2005; Marcuse, 1972). The perpetuation of institutionalized discrimination in the pipelines of the higher education system has been historically prevalent (Anderson, 1992; Apple, 1998; IROPA, 2010; Marcuse, 1972; NCES, 2010; Ollman; 1998; Pinar, 2005). The manifestation of such discrimination emphasizes the financial gains made by corporate markets through the promotion of mainstream knowledge. This has consistently had a negative impact on educational institutions, their statistical trends reveal evolving completion and success rate deficiencies for Racially Stigmatized Identities (Anderson, 1992; Apple, 1998; IROPA, 2010; Marcuse, 1972; NCES, 2010; Ollman; 1998; Pinar, 2005). Apple's research revealed the manifestation of discrimination in education and the current state of curriculum and how these have been constructed to serve industrial and economic needs, as reflected through standardization, systems management – this is politically dishonest (Apple, 1992, 1996, 2006; Apple &

Beyer, 1998). The conflict itself is rooted in views of race, class, and gender justice that prevent a serious analysis of education needed to understand students' struggles by examining the way the educational system operates. This maneuver is meant to protect and preserve an authoritarian populist fundamentalist tradition of middle and upper class White Christian males and their axiological, epistemological, phenomenological, and ontological existence (Apple, 2000).

The Experience of Black Students in Higher Education

Bell (1987), Delgado (1989), Jost et al. (2005), and Solórzano and Yosso (2002) illustrate the necessity to analyze, teach, and furnish a critical understanding of intersectional experiences' influence on actions affecting Black students' progress in post-secondary institutions. Astin (1982), Masurky (1997), and others studies showed that students dropping out is a clear indication that society as a whole and educational institutions in particular do not provide for the welfare of all its student citizenry (Chávez et al., 1991; Vann Lynch, 2002; Watson, 1994). Furthermore, this research addresses the issue of attrition and its relation to student achievement with regard to elements of academic and social intergration, as well Black students and their negative experiences with campus administration. For example, studies by Casey (2004), Cooper et al. (2006), and Lynch (2002) all found that increased success of Black students in education is related to higher education institutions promoting Black student socialization, contribution, cultural relevance, and the presence of faculty of color.

With regard to the lack of faculty of color, the NCES (2010) reported that Racially Stigmatized Identities account for less than 5% of professors in both public and private educational institutions and Black faculty comprise less than 2%. Delgado and Bernal (2000) and Vann Lynch (2002) revealed a contextual analysis that asserts that without a balance and strong presence of faculty of color, there remains a lack of cultural diversity in academia. These two studies highlight the absence of such a faculty of color and how it creates a deficient space in education for students of color, a lack of experiential and legitimate knowledge within the academic and administrative foundations of such campuses.

Vann Lynch's (2002) study revealed that when students feel socially, academically, culturally, and politically invisible in higher education institutions, it negatively impacts their retention rates. Lynch and Delgado and Bernal's research incorporated the counter story to share a non-traditional epistemological perspective of experiential narratives that are legitimate for research practices. The research paradigms of critical race theory and Black feminism allow a point of analysis for political and hegemonic, conscious or unconscious, discriminatory structures that disadvantage students of color, especially Black and Latino students in educational institutions (Fine, 1991;Yosso & Ceja, 2000). Fine (1991) changed the perspective of student retention in education from the dropout to the pushout and explored the influence of institutional political structures. Matsuda et al. (1993) and Solórzano et al. (2000) support the findings emphasized in Fine's work, using their research to evaluate the educational experience of Black students through an analysis of educational institutions' usage of race and racism as political instruments that build on the pushout rate of students of color. The research findings examine the lack of enforcement of not only legal processes but also the presence of privilege that overshadows due process concerning students of color, especially Black students. These studies evaluated legal and historical battles which Racially Stigmatized Identities undertook to gain positive cultural recognition in educational institutions in the face of social injustice. The studies also reported multiple and frequent blatant racial macro and microaggressions faced by Black students on predominantly White college campuses and the lack of administrative and legal protection present to address this form of discrimination (Ceja et al., 2000; Matsuda et al., 1993). The issue in the research is not just that discrimination is put at the forefront but also the lack of alternatives and possible solutions to deal with discriminatory actions on college campuses, leaving students with a sense of rejection and powerlessness against dominant forces.

Valencia (1997, 2010) dissected educational inequalities and their constructions through a deficit model of thinking and the practices that displace the cultural richness of students of color and their correlation with educational requirements. Valencia positions the manifestation of constructions that promote the belief that there is a cultural inferiority, especially in the value of education, among Racially Stigmatized

Identities as compared to the dominant ideology of whiteness. Valencia (2010) and Smith-Maddox and Solórzano's (2002) research critically evaluated the structures within educational institutions through a historical lens, analyzing the discriminatory actions in enrollment procedures, policy formation, and other educational practices towards people of color. The research also explained that racialized institutions create racialized actions, which in turn perpetuate multiple forms of discrimination against marginalized student populations. Astin (1982), Cejaet al. (2000), Watson (1994), and Yosso (2005) called for an imperative investigation into the dominant culture's ability to assess the capital of marginal groups in terms of educational contribution. Margins asserted throughout the investigation a substantial need for a critical reflection of power, which involves the analysis of the cause and effect, which in my research become the "who", "what", "how", and the "why" that relate to Black students' retention rates.

The NCES (2006, 2010) conducted federal research that revealed Black students' enrollment percentages into higher educational institutions have increased; however, the same research showed that the national graduation rates for these students remained consistently low within the same institutions (NCES, 2006, 2010). The NCES studies, performed by federal agencies, illustrate a dramatic completion inconsistency within the educational pipeline. The NCES showed that students of color are indeed enrolling in higher educational institutions at increasing rates and a proportion are completing their degree programs. The report also reveals statistics that could lead to a deficit of students

49

of color, such as high rates of Black and Latino students attending public schools considered low-income serving (Title I) and high-poverty primary and secondary public schools. The issue with the information presented in this report does not lie in the degree of accuracy but the fact that the information is incomplete, which creates a deficit of poor and impoverished students, especially those of color (Moll et al., 2005).

The Pursuit of Education: Black Students Diminishing Through Three Cracks in the Educational Pipeline

Post-secondary educational institutions are producing alarming incompletion rates of Black students; this is also a problem at the secondary level of education. Alon and Tienda (2005), Cross and Slater(2001), and Yosso (2005) highlighted that cultural inclusion in secondary education is an important contributing factor in the enrollment decisions of Black students and other students of color. Yosso (2005) and the U.S. Census (2000) outlined the structure of the educational pipeline; Yosso's work breaks down the experiences of Chicana/o students and faculty in relation to the educational pipeline. Throughout the model of the pipeline, there is an invisible linear structure of White supremacy built on the premise of White privilege historically founded on the evolution of slavery, acceptance of integration, the transcendence of race consciousness, and what is known as the social progression of equality (Bell, 1992; Hooks, 1981; Perry; 1995). This model presents a basic overview of the educational process, but as explained by Yosso (2005), the pipeline does not reveal the cracks students of color fall through or

50

must navigate within the pipeline. The works of Bell, Hooks, and Yosso share counter stories that relay the historical discriminatory treatment of Blacks and the critical navigational skills of Chicana/o students in post-secondary education as a means of academic survival. The counter stories demonstrate critical commonalities such as racial discrimination, its substantial negative impact on the progress of both groups, especially in education. The model of the educational pipeline displayed by the U.S. Census Bureau, evaluated by Yosso, identifies the process and multiple levels of educational structures in the American educational system. Bell (1992), Feagin and Sikes (1994), Feagin and Sean (1998), Hooks (1981), and Marable (2006) have evaluated stages of racialized pain and educational procedures that perpetuate scars of oppression and produce a ripple effect of intellectual scarring and the intersectional discrimination against students of color throughout this pipeline. Institutional structures must include spaces to incorporate counter stories as an analytical framework to employ the experiences of people of color, especially in the educational pipeline, as a transformative method of education. Educational institutions need critical race theory and Black feminism as methodologies to create a political voice for marginalized students, especially for Black students engulfed in the political and pedagogical practices of secondary and post-secondary educational institutions. Garibaldi (1984, 1996) and Whiting (2009) showed that in order to ensure that more Black students enter the college pipeline, secondary education must develop strategies to facilitate the graduation of a larger number of Black students by incorporating more inclusive curricular and pedagogical spaces for students to share experiential discourses. The studies completed by Delgado Bernal (2000) and De'Souza (1991) not only emphasize the importance of experiential knowledge but also a discourse to legitimize the content of these epistemological experiences. Davis (1994) and Fredua-Kwarteng (2005) addressed the institutional discrimination faced by Black and African students that revealed that instructional methods in secondary educational institutions promote a sense of powerlessness, emotional torture, and trivialization of Black intellect. The fact that Black students are not able to share their cultural, racial, and ethnic experiences and associate them with their learning environment impacts their educational experience. These studies explain that a dialogue with the inclusion of multiple perspectives is needed; it must enable a discourse that addresses race in relation to power structures and begins to frame and confront the issue, especially of the marginalized and oppressed, which, in the case of this research, would be the cultural richness of Black students.

Crack #1: The Definition of American Citizenship and Racial Assimilation in Education

Delgado and Stefanic (2001) explain the myth of meritocracy and the false promotion of the idea that if every individual attends school, works hard, and becomes a dedicated citizen of the United States, anyone can achieve success, academic or economic, in essence that the American dream is attainable. Bell (1987), Collins (2000),

Kendall (2006), Rothenberg (2002), and Yancy (2004) found that this myth does not account for the assimilation of Racially Stigmatized Identities to White privileged culture, marginalization, isolation, and segregation, enforced by political policies and actions that inflict the unspoken part of this myth. The myth of meritocracy is a paradigmatic manifestation of White supremacy that overlooks the mythical existence of equality and success in our educational system (Peller, 1995). Assimilation into White privileged culture is supported by the post-secondary educational process. A social reconstruction of education using critical race theory and tenets of Black feminism, perspectives, and methods of a transformational approach call for the inclusion of social justice and a multicultural curriculum within educational institutions, as well as a critical experiential analysis of race and education within post-secondary educational institutions (Maddox & Smith, 2002; Zeichner, 1991).

Hardwood, Hunt, and Mendenhall (2010) tracked the occurrences of racial microaggressions on Black students in college campuses from their White counterparts and how it affects the completion rate of students of color.[4] Davis (1994) demonstrated that one of the salient contributors to the performance of Black students in

---

[4] See Swim, J., Hyers, L. L., Cohen, L. L., Fitzgerald, D. C., & Bylsma, W. H. (2003) *African American college students experiences with everyday racism: Characteristics of and responses to these incidents. Journal of Black Psychology.* This article provided a counter story of Black students' experiences and their everyday battles with racism in dealing with staff, prejudiced statements, and expressions in European American Institutions and these incidents' effect on their emotional and social lives as well as their completion rate. See also Solórzano et al. in (FN13).

predominantly White institutions is the lack of social and academic support provided by the university. Studies by Davis (1994) and Hardwood et al. (2010) investigated Black students' post-secondary experience. They found that the racial climate in the campus influences both academic and social oppression faced by Black students at the hands of their non-Black peers and professors. These studies contain the indirect testimony of Black students' accounts offering a representation of the world that can truly be developed by the counter story. Ladson-Billings (1995), Collins (2000), and Sólorzano (2000) found that inequalities form a logical and predictable result of a racialized society in which discussions of race and racism continue to be muted and marginalized. The silencing of Blacks in education due to the belief that they must assimilate to dominant White cultural standards of educational success and learning has been expressed by King (1991); this is a form of dyconscious racism, a powerful force that embeds the thought process of both students and educators in educational institutions.

Feagin and Sikes (1995) described embedded forces; this refers to the public post-secondary institutions and their policies that affect cultural groups and the political practices exhibited by these institutions. The research involved interviewing Black students in predominantly White institutions and found that upon arrival on campus, assimilation imposed on these students is prominent. The idea of assimilation is not the same as integration; there is a lack of equity and acceptance of what cultural values and practices students will bring into the campus atmosphere. The studies also define and show the impact of ingrained racist practices by defining the embedding of racism associated with not only the size and relevance of systematic political structures in the institutions but also the groups that are marginalized (Feagin & Eckberg, 1980; Feagin & Sikes, 1995). DeCuir and Dixson (2004) and Ladson-Billings and Tate (1995) explained how the educational assimilation of Black students into the dominant culture's capital became a proficient practice of educational institutions that must be reconstructed. The non-incorporation of cultural and social backgrounds denies students equitable opportunities to express part of their epistemological being and contributes negatively to their educational experience, creating a crack in the educational pipeline, a crack that evolves due to an educational process of cultural assimilation and elimination (Delpit, 2010; King, 1991; Yosso, 2005).

Cullen (2004), Keller (1998), and Haynes Writer (2010) address the definition of American citizenship using educational means to promote obedience through ideologies of patriotism and citizenship. According to Cullen and Keller, the American way was designed by early scholars and politicians who were Anglo-Saxon Americans, belonging to upper- and middle-class , who epitomized the "model citizen". The concept of the model citizen has historically emphasized the ideas of individualism, laissez faire, and ownership of private property (Cullen, 2004; Kullen, 1988). These works also explain the history of classism and racism that preluded and pre-shadowed the American way of life, a reflection of pedagogic action in our educational institutions that promoted

55

symbolic violence[5] towards the cultural significance of people of color. Haynes Writer (2010) stated that the goal of our educational institutions is to produce dedicated citizens by teaching a White mainstream elitist curriculum. Apple (1996, 1998), Pinar (2005), and Sleeter (2001) support Writer's statement by demonstrating that in order to succeed in this environment, students need to consume the White elite mainstream knowledge imposed on them; they are required to abide by White-mandated policies and rules. The ideology of a right-winged perspective defining knowledge illegitimatizes the experiential knowledge and creates a deficit of the educational value and experiences of Black students while also subtly incorporating academic and social assimilation into the educational pipeline (Apple, 1998; Pinar, 2005).

Ladson-Billings (2009) and Collins (2000) explained the deficit perspective imposed on experiential knowledge and the potential of such knowledge to provide an alternate perspective into the lives of people of color.[6] This perspective epitomizes Black students as second-class students and creates ethos to address the cultural

---

[5] See Bourdieu & Passeron. (2000). *Reproduction in education, society, and culture.* Symbolic violence represented through pedagogic action addresses the delimitation objectively enacted by imposing and inculcating certain meanings, treated by selection and the corresponding exclusion as worthy of being reproduced by PA, which reproduces (in both senses) the arbitrary selection a group or class objectively makes in and through cultural arbitrary (Bourdieu & Passeron, 2000).

[6] See for example, Bernal and Villalpando (2002), *An Apartheid of Knowledge in Academia: The Struggle over Legitimate Knowledge.* This work addresses culture through the counter stories of faculty of color in higher education institutions. Further, Bell Hooks and Cornell West, *Breaking Bread* (1991). Bell Hooks, *Ain't I a Woman: Black Women and Feminism* (1981). These works take into account the historical context of the experience of Black people within the community and the validity behind their cultural beliefs and experiences. These works address personal experiences as well as the counter perspective of Black life and the importance of historical events that have led to the cultural depravity of Black people.

depravity and the bias of legitimate knowledge in higher education (Bernal & Villalpando, 2002; Ladson-Billings, 2009). The literature speaks of the value of cultural capital based on whiteness and its ability to exclude other forms of cultural knowledge. Sleeter and Grant (1986), Sleeter (2005), and Banks and Banks (2004) state that in order to gain an accurate understanding of the occurrences in educational institutions, educators must consider the intersectional impacts of race, class, and gender on educational equity. In the documentary *Race: The Story We Tell* produced by Alderman (2003), the ideology of the American way of life was evaluated as a form of symbolic violence, because historically, the American way of life was founded on the hard work of Black and Latino ancestry as well as other subordinated groups and the mistreatment of those populations. The historical treatment of Racially Stigmatized Identities justifies the American way of life and the exclusion and critical contributions in the areas of social, economic, and lingual development of such populations to the American educational system; these contributions are being pushed through the cracks of the educational pipeline (Aldeman, 2003; Rubin, 2004; Haynes Writer, 2010). This research provides a critical lens for the thought and language of multiple cultures and the way in which they enhance and fulfill a much needed pedagogical and curricular requirement in learning environments within the educational pipeline. Implications within Marable's (2006) work examine racial stratification and the protection, manufacturing, and augmentation of mainstream knowledge in educational institutions to protect and enhance the status and beliefs of White elitist groups. Critical race theorists and Black feminists state that the experiences of Racially Stigmatized Identities are crucial in educational institutions and offer learning possibilities that would otherwise be unavailable to teachers and learners; they further state that in order to adequately achieve such knowledge, we must explore the effects of institutionalized racism (Bernal & Villalpando, 2002; Collins, 2004; Hooks, 1994).

Bourdieu and Passeron (2000), Collins (2004), and Valenzuela (1999) frame administrative procedure, curriculum, and instructional practices in educational institutions and create a context that illustrates education's dependability on the dominant culture's capital, the culture of White elitist Christian males, reflective of an upper-class society. This literature examines the dominant cultures' perspective of society and explains the dominance of one story, one that substantially engulfs racial limitations on the ideologies that define knowledge and success. The literature reveals the assumption that minority communities possess no cultural wealth or capital. Consequently, educational institutions hold onto the belief that their structures must "help" students whose race class, and background has left them lacking the necessary knowledge, social skills, abilities, and cultural capital. Within the curricular and instructional, cultural assumptions and a one-sided bias, there are limitations of entrapment of the voice and experiences in the counter stories of those populations, in my study, Black students. The language of the counter story has to be inclusive in education. Counter storytelling offers a particular account of the world. The power in the narration is a reflection that addresses issues of racism, marginalization, and other forms of oppression excluded in majoritarian stories (Sólorzano & Yosso, 2002). Without the inclusion of counter stories to aid in the structures of the educational pipeline, there remains a discriminatory boundary and multiple metaphorical cracks through which students of color fall.

Crack #2: Curricular Cracks of Epistemological Subordination in Education

Curriculum theorists such as Apple (2000) and Pinar (2004) address the ideology of mainstream knowledge and its structural impact within educational institutions. Their evaluations bring to light right-wing political positions strategically residing in the educational pipeline. Their evaluations and analysis of curriculum has shown that the standardizing of curriculum is indeed creating a crack in the educational pipeline. Hooks and West (1991) and Marable (2006) evaluated the displacement of Blacks and provided a perspective on the deference of marginalized, oppressed groups and their underemphasized curricular cultural contributions to learning environments of educational institutions. What this research has demonstrated is a result of historical White elitist political ideologies that lead to discriminatory practices in curriculum formation; there is an exclusion of the epistemological contributions of people of color.

Michael Apple (1998) stated that the concern for curriculum must reside with the connections between our educational institutions and differential cultural, political, and economic power (p. 5). He also reflected on the number crunchers of education and believed that all too many researchers could still be characterized by the phrase coined years ago by C. Wright Mills, "abstract empiricists" (Apple, 2006). The issue Apple lies in the priority of the evaluators of education and their lack of potential to pay attention to other cultural factors that affect student progress. His belief reflects that the current state of curriculum is constructed for the purpose of industrial and economic need reflected through standardization, systems management, and is thus politically dishonest (Apple & Beyer, 1998). Apple (1998, 2006) and Pinar (1975, 2003, 2004, 2009) both criticize institutions such as research and development agencies, academics in higher education, and federal departments, asserting that they impose on the learning capacity of "underprivileged populations", such as women and people of color. The literature reveals that educational institutions, by inflicting their own curricular privileges on student populations, have been rejecting the cultural richness of Black students historically, socially, and politically through subtle discriminatory practices.

Astin (1971), Allen (1992), Masurky (1997), and Cross and Slater (2001) demonstrated a progressive issue that Black students attribute to their push-out rate, that is, the rejection they face in a social system within education that renders them invisible. The studies of Allen, Astin, Masurky, and Cross and Slater bring to the surface the lack of social and academic integration of Black students within higher education and address similar patterns within secondary education. Data in these studies redirects traditional evaluations of educational research and challenges in educational objectives in including epistemological contributions within secondary and post-secondary education. Inglis (1988) and Kumashiro (2004, 2008) found that right-wing political powers within education are culturally insensitive to the problems faced by students in educational institutions. This research analyzed an elitist model with performance measures that evaluate and support high-performing students in education. In this research, there was a contextualizing of what Inglis referred to as the hunters and gatherers of social numbers and the way in which the importance of quantitative data allows policy makers to remain unconnected to the relations of inequalities that surround them in our educational institutions. The research brings to light the issue of excessive promotion of science and technology and the disproportionate amount of resources allocated to advance students of color in educational institutions. The extensive emphasis on science in education creates a lack of focus on societal issues such as poverty, crime, and other social problems that affect oppressed and marginalized populations.

Pinar (2005) and Sleeter (2001, 2005) stated that a reconceptualization of educational practices, including curriculum and pedagogy, are important. There is a deep insensitivity toward the cultural existence of students in the educational practice of

61

White elitist edifications. Educators must be willing to dialogically involve students in educational learning. William Pinar's research (1975, 1976, 1992, 2004) reminded educational institutions to not forget humanization and not define it in terms of White elite norms, or what he refers to as traditionalist norms, because such a practice elicits intersectional discrimination, producing curricular cracks in education. This research showed that within their educational methods, educators and policy makers must be willing to have discussions based on what makes people uncomfortable, especially on topics of race, class, and gender. In supporting the theory of educational practices critically evaluated by Pinar, Christine Sleeter (2001, 2004, 2005) suggests that we as a society do not do a very good job of educating students from diverse populations. In fact, not only do we deficit such populations through our educational practices by defining them in terms of low achievers, we eliminate potential academic progress through practices influenced by such beliefs. Sleeter's findings state that within the educational curriculum, there is a lack of content related to diversity and equity, where differences are viewed as a potential problem. She emphasized the undervaluation of accumulated knowledge and the overvaluation of mainstream knowledge in education, causing the curriculum to become a part of a selective tradition (Sleeter, 2001, 2005).

Moll et al. (2004) and Sleeter (2005) reinforced that by integrating student learning processes from within the home into the curriculum and classroom practices, educators can help students gain new knowledge more effectively. Sleeter (2005), Apple

62

(1998), and Pinar (2005) addressed the epistemological influences on curriculum, by asking the question whose knowledge is most important and why. These three theorists considered cultural authoritarianism in curriculum formation which promotes a corporate marketed standardized perspective; this enforces the societal preparation of students and the subordination of cultural capital of students from marginalized backgrounds.

Furthermore, Apple (1998), Pinar (2005, 2004), and Valencia (2010) believed that higher education has become an epitome of number crunching that duplicates a corporatized model that has infiltrated the holistic and empowering purpose of education. The conflict in education is rooted in restricted views of race, class, and gender justice. These prevent a serious analysis of education that is needed to view the ongoing struggles of students through the privilege of education. The literatures examines White male privilege ideologies in which social justice is not present – these are practices of an operation meant to protect and preserve an authoritarian, populist, fundamentalist tradition of middle- and upper-class White Christian males that promote their cultural prestige (Apple, 2000; Astin, 1971). These texts by Astin and Apple, though decades apart, assert that education, especially post-secondary, has become a promotion system based on status which also affects the selection process of Black students into such ideologically based institutions. The studies not only address intersectional discriminatory acts but also highlight claims that support the view that

63

education has become a biased cultural system arranged for competition and status. Ayers, Quinn, and Stovall (2009) and Banks (1985) explained that social justice in education should uphold pillars of equity, activism, and social literacy. In a revolutionary and rigorous way, these would value the importance of cultural relevance, the nourishing nature of educational experiences, and awareness about multicultural populations that coexist within post-secondary educational institutions.

According to critical race theorists and Black feminist studies by Collins (2000), Delgado and Stefanic (2001), Mickelson and Smith (2004), Moore (2004), and Villalpando and Bernal (2002), there is an emphasis that confronts legitimate versus experiential epistemologies and the foundation to impose the belief of meritocracy. These insightful positionalities within critical race theory and Black feminism offer paradigms, perspectives, and curricular methods that incorporate transformational approaches to the structural and cultural aspects of educational policies and practices. These studies call for an integration of students of color, especially Black students, into the academic and social processes of higher education institutions.

Kendall (2006) stated that education offered through dominant White elitist ideologies and beliefs is an injustice to ethnic, non-White students and promotes inequities through educational practices, also known as the process of "othering". Taylor et al. (2009) delved in epistemological concepts of both deficit thinking and racist ideologies embedded in the everyday rhythms of internal and external structures in the

64

educational pipeline which students need to successfully navigate (Bell, 1992; Collins, 2000; Delgado & Stefanic, 2001). The internal and external structures explained within these studies are not only limited to the current conditions that discriminate against Black students in education but also historical occurrences. Anderson (1989), Anderson and Herr (1993), Kelly and Gaskell (1996), and Marshall (1991) transcended beyond the classroom to ask questions about the historical forces that shaped societal patterns as well as fundamental issues and dilemmas of power, policy, and dominance in educational institutions. Exclusionary acts toward Racially Stigmatized Identities in educational institutions are justified by conservative politicized policies that create vulnerability and a mainstream curriculum that perpetuates underachievement through accountability and overshadows racist cultural politics of educational authoritarianism (Banks, 2004; Bell, 1992; Pinar, 2005). Kaplan et al.(2002) and Irvine (1990) explained that numerous teachers attribute inaccurate characterizations of both behavior and academic ability to students based on race and ethnicity.

Bell et al.(1998) examined a definition of educational success that has established a misguided meaning and purpose of education. The belief is that success is achieved when students in the educational system complete their education and participate in an industrial and technological society supported by the working class. The literature explains that as citizens, one must abide by rules created by a right wing government, one that constructs educational procedures with the intention of advancing capitalism (Collins, 2000; Rubin, 2004). Collins and Robin also explained the absence of cultural inclusion in defining success and productivity in the processes dictated by political structures in the educational pipeline. Hooks (1994) and Oesterreich (2007) offered a broader understanding of young men and women with culturally relevant research through the theoretical frameworks of Black feminism. The research stated the need for knowledge that educators bring to their pedagogy, policies, and research to inevitably connect both spiritually and culturally with the students, when they are teaching with the aim to promote actual educational success.

Crack #3: Discrimination in the Representation of Educational Leadership in the Higher Educational Pipeline

Gosetti et al. (1991) and Irwin and Pinar (2005) critically analyzed the context in which educational institutions define leadership, stating that it is problematic. These authors found that what students read in textbooks, what they hear and see during lectures, is not an accurate definition of leadership as there is an omission of leadership figures of color in the curriculum. Irwin and Pinar highlighted multiple examples of the encounters students in post-secondary educational institutions and throughout the educational pipeline that indicate an absence in representation of diverse leadership, even though students of color constitute almost 50% of students in primary and secondary educational institutions. The representation of educational leadership in these studies portrayed a White elite model of political and historical figures in leadership

66

positions. The NCES (1990, 2000, 2010) and the U. S. Census Bureau (2000, 2010)

reported that a majority of low and extreme poverty elementary and secondary schools

contain a majority of children of color, predominantly Black and Latino children; this

has been a consistent and historical trend in education. These reports also prove that a

majority of educators and administrators within such primary, secondary, and post-

secondary institutions are not Racially Stigmatized Identities and are in fact White

(NCES, 1990, 2000, 2010).

According to Mitchell et al., attributions of leadership by observers and group

members are biased by their individual realities (Bass, 1984). These realities described

by Mitchell et al. and Bass describe procedures in educational institutions that render

people of color, especially Blacks, and women almost invisible in educational leadership

positions. The research continues to evaluate the way in which we define leadership and

how it is constructed through a bias based on the dominant group's historical

perspective. This perspective has created a societal norm that revolves around an

extremely White male elitist hegemonic ideal of how leadership is viewed and

categorized. The research indicated that the problem in leadership construction within

education is a lack of promotion of individuals from different intersectional categories

based on race, class, and gender. Crenshaw (2001) explained that in order to liberate

one's self and systems of discriminatory discursive representations, we must begin to liberate structures like the educational pipeline by resisting dominant perceptions, especially those that build on the premise of defining leadership.

Paulo Freire (1996) stated that the process of liberating human beings and treating them as humans is a phenomenon that cannot be achieved by semi humans. If the portrayals of leadership are centered on the foundation of a dominant elite ideology and eradicate the importance and strengths of oppressed populations, we are treating such figures as semi humans. His works also analyze the concept of dehumanization and how it makes power irrelevant in the eyes of the marginalized and oppressed groups and more obtainable to those in privileged positions (Friere, 1970, 1996, 1997). According to this work, morality, nurturing, and empathy must be considered when utilizing power in developing effective educational leadership traits.

Apple (1990,1992), Ladson-Billings (2009), Pinar (2004), and Sleeter (1992, 2005) discussed transformative approaches to curriculum in education that imminently lead to the success of oppressed and marginalized populations, especially people of color; this requires going against mainstream curricular concepts and incorporating multicultural educational practices throughout the curriculum in the educational pipeline. The content of this research calls for a reformation of curriculum through transformative intellectual knowledge of recollection and basic understanding, prediction and synthesis of ideas, and evaluation of the current curriculum in place within educational institutions (Sleeter, 2005; Hooks, 1991; Collins, 2000). Sleeter

(2005) declared that in order for such a reevaluation to occur, those in educational leadership positions, such as teachers, administrators, and curriculum designers must create approaches in their praxis that incorporate a theoretical integration of life experiences, student engagement, and rise in the awareness of issues faced by people of color. This praxis creates a catalyst for change in the classroom. Praxis within education administration has to incorporate a presence of student communal knowledge. Ladson-Billings (1995, 2009) and Moll et al. (2004) emphasized the importance of funds of knowledge and cultural wealth provided by underserved populations and marginalized communities within an educational institution through teaching practices (Sleeter, 2005). These scholars not only furnish examples of the incorporation of communal knowledge, they also show that it is engaging and beneficial for students of color in educational institutions. Substantial power within teacher leadership must maintain efforts built to promote social justice for the communities in which they teach and for the children belonging to these communities (Moll et al., 2004; Sleeter, 2005). The opportunities teachers and other educational leaders possess, who understand the importance of communal knowledge in relation to the navigation of students within the educational pipeline, is critical to student completion within institutions of higher education (Yosso, 2005).

Middlehurst (2008) opined that leadership is viewed as a social construct, a reflection of epistemological teachings that differs across cultural and educational contexts. This discourse of leadership roles and the responsibilities of teachers and administrators in educational institutions challenges educational leaders to incorporate equitable and socially just practices in positions of leadership. If educational leaders cannot accomplish this task, then they become oppressors, as they are not engaged in the struggle for the liberation of their students' identities and right to learn. They have to realize teaching is not just the transfer of knowledge from teacher to student (Freire, 1996, 1998). Educational leaders have to be willing to empower and liberate their students from mainstream knowledge through the incorporation of new knowledges that are experiential and diverse. Historical data ranging from Astin (1968) to Jost et al. (2005) illustrated that in order for educators to begin this type of liberation, they must first reexamine the presence of institutionalized discrimination and then begin reconstructing educational outcomes and selection procedures in multiple layers of higher education (Astin, 1968, 1971; Feagin & Sykes, 1995; Feagin & Eckberg, 1980; Kantrowitz, 2011).

Summarizing the curricular cracks in higher education requires an evaluation of the practices and procedures that take place within these institutions. The chart below identifies a summary of the issues and supportive research identified within this section of the literature review. The objective of this chart is to create a foundation that will be later developed after the research in this study has been conducted and analyzed.

Table 1

70

	Crack #1: Defining American Citizenship and Racial Assimilation in Education	Crack #2: Curricular Cracks of Epistemological Subordination in Education	Crack #3: Discrimination in the Representation of Educational Leadership in the Pipeline
Academic Support	Political practices that promote the idea of assimilation while enhancing exclusionary practices toward the potential of Black students and the richness of their cultural contributions (Dixon, 2004; Feagin & Sykes, 1995).	The standardization of curriculum has leaked into higher education, pushing forth a right wing agenda of economic progression engulfed in technological and scientific epistemologies, strategically deleting and overshadowing spaces of curriculum that embrace Black students' historical, social, and political contributions (Astin, 1971; Allen, 1992; Cross & Slater, 2001; Masurky, 1997).	The problem in leadership construction within education is the shortage of promotion of individuals who possess intersectional differences in the categories based on race, class, and gender (Gosetti et al., 1991; Irwin & Pinar, 2005). A non-representation of Black presence in educational leadership positions has been shown to contribute to early departure from such institutions

			(Masurky, 1997; Tinto, 2002)
Social Support	Educational institutions must provide a source of social support in the areas of guidance, counseling, mentoring, and ethnic student centers (Tinto, 2002; Van Lynch, 2002).	Insufficient educational secondary preparation of low-income and first-generation college students and enhanced need for deficit labels such as remedial and differentiating between students by faculty and administration in higher education (Rendon, 1994; Solórzano et al., 2000)	Social integration plays a key role in the success of students in higher education; the engagement of Black students involves multicultural educational techniques and concepts in the construction of educational policies, practices, and pedagogies (Astin, 1993; Ladson-Billings, 2009; Tinto, 1993).

Mismatching: The Practice of Blaming the Victim

Alon and Tienda (2005), Cross (1993), and Journal of Blacks in Higher Education (2002) (2001) correlate the post-secondary choices of Black college students with their low graduation rates. This research proposed that the low graduation rate of Black students in post-secondary educational institutions contributed to students' need to attend colleges where their academic credentials corresponded with the institutional average. Significantly, the results indicated that the post-secondary choice of Black students was a huge risk factor for college failure. The issue within these studies is the analysis of the researchers who maintain HBCU's stance in nurturing Black students' academic and social needs. Harper (2004), Pope (2009), and Journal of Blacks in Higher Education (2001, 2002) showed that over two-thirds of Black students attending HBCU did not graduate; HBCU's overall graduation rate was nationally lower than other post-secondary institutions. The purpose of the research was to provide an alternative approach to tackling Black students' dropout rate. Significant dynamics overlooked by Alon and Tienda and Cross were socially just practices and/or malpractices of educational institutions that hinder the completion rate of Black students. Researchers such as Carey (2005), Cokely (2000), Malveaux (2005), and Pascarella and Terenzini (1991) forwarded opposing views that measure the impact institutions have on the social and academic progress of Black students after they arrive on campus rather than the type of institutions they attend. These studies addressed not only the psychosocial experiences of students but also the formulation of curriculum to produce positive

student outcomes within post-secondary settings. One primary point presented within

these studies is the non-deficit focus of Black students and their willingness to pursue

success in post-secondary educational institutions (Rowley, 2000). However, drawing

such conclusions without considering student willingness to succeed and excel entails

overlooking a broader capitalistic system designed to demote the progress of Blacks by

constructing discriminatory social, economic, and historical structures (Collins &

Anderson, 2000; Hooks, 1981; Delgado & Stefanic, 2001; Marcuse, 1972; Matsuda et

al., 1993; Ollman, 1998). Collins and Anderson (2000), Ladson-Billings and Tate

(1995), and Delgado and Stefanic (2001) stated that race matters and methodologies

such as critical race theory and Black feminism are needed to critically evaluate systems

that would prefer to present alternative fictitious narratives.

Counter Storytelling in Research Methodology

Critical race theory and Black feminist methodologies provide the use of

theoretical frameworks as part of an evolving research construct and are critical

frameworks that develop an understanding of marginal populations through the

perspective of those populations, which constitutes the counter story[7]. When conducting

---

[7] See Patricia Hill-Collins, *Race Class and Gender* (2004) which addresses simultaneous intersection of
systems between race, class, and gender. She stated that all Racially Stigmatized Identities at some
time in their lives experience racism and that racism is framed by an overlap of systems of race, class,
and gender. The subjectivity of race relies on the multiple experiences that Racially Stigmatized
Identities face as a result of institutional racism (Collins, 2004, p. 85). See Derrick Bell (1992), *Faces*

research on race, racism, and other forms of inequitable actions, one must incorporate the counter story in order to present a socially just perspective (Solórzano & Delgado Bernal, 2001; Solórzano & Yosso, 2000, 2001, 2002). Ladson-Billings (2000) stated that racialized discourses and ethnic epistemologies are forms of counter stories that allow space in research to investigate the contingency of the mind in relation to others outside intersections. The process of the counter story includes a cultural interpretation which strategically positions testimony as an intellectual discourse by interrelating experiential forms of knowledge (Autumn, 1985; Graham, 2000; Mishler, 2010). Weiner (2003) explained that testimony provides a default justification which does not depend on other beliefs but is ultimately based on the believer's past and current experiences. In Black feminisms, testimony is grounded as a story of survival that implicates oppression, marginality, and exploitation which raises consciousness through personal narration. The evidence in testimony cannot rely strictly on what has been told by the narrator, in this case, the participant. The justification for the acceptance of testimony in this study is supported by scholarly research, predominantly critical race theory and Black feminism.

---

at the Bottom of the Well, Chapter 5, *Divining a Racial Realism Theory*, which addresses politicized racism and discrimination through law. Matsuda et al. (1993), in *Words that Wound*, speaks about the structural reality of racism to keep selected victim groups in subordinate positions (pp. 22–23).

Delgado (1989) incorporated counter storytelling as a method to relate the untold stories of marginalized populations, as a tool for analyzing and challenging the stories of those in power and whose story is a natural part of the dominant majoritarian discourse (Solórzano & Yosso, 2002). Delgado's research explains that students of color need a discourse to share their history, culture, and backgrounds through counter storytelling, which would allow epistemological, axiological, phenomenological, and ontological learning possibilities. Black feminists state that all experiences are political in some context (Collins, 2000; Hooks, 1981, 1984). Black feminisms and critical race theory provide a theoretical lens that emphasizes a call to action to investigate and measure the impact of practices of post-secondary institutions and the way in which these affect the educational experience of Black students.

Conclusion

The aim of this chapter was to provide an extensive review of literature explaining the social and academic dynamics of education that informed my research. I also incorporated the theoretical frameworks of Black feminism and critical race theory in relation to the educational experiences and retention rate of Black students in higher education. Throughout this section, I discussed issues within the educational pipeline, administrative practices in relation to the social and academic foundations of post-secondary educational institutions. The chapter concludes with a brief introduction to the study's methodology.

Chapter III

Methods

Introduction

This chapter introduces the rationale behind the qualitative research methodology for the study, both theoretical and applied. The methods of data collection and research design with qualitative methodologies that give life to the research study have been included. This chapter also contains the important constructs of validity and trustworthiness achieved through the process of crystallization; my position and role as a researcher and the importance of remaining true to my research participants and methods used in the study have been described in order to comprehend the data collected.

Rationale for Qualitative Research

Qualitative research provides a transformative practice by allowing the fundamental interpretation of Black student voice that has the potential to form an organic counter story through the power of the participants' words and increasingly critical perspective of the many educational practices (some of which might be oppressive) in post-secondary institutions (Lutrell, 2009; Marshall & Rossman, 2011; Mills, 2009). Qualitative research enables the researcher to investigate phenomena involving Black students without drawing conclusions that may deficit the stories of Racially Stigmatized Identities (Smith-Maddox & Solórzano, 2002; Solórzano &

Yosso, 2002). Moreover, qualitative research allows the participants to provide a collaborative and deep-rooted, clear-cut understanding of the experiences that construct the over-arching phenomena of the research study (Lutrell, 2009; Marshall & Rossman, 2011). A transformative practice in research must be supported by transformational research methodologies.

Rationale for Case Study

The qualitative inquiry employed in this research is case study. Case study in qualitative research does not comprise a methodology alone but allows the holistic and analytical potential of data collected to be measured organically, hermeneutically, permitting the examination of participants' cultural practices as well as any systematic structure that need to be studied (Stake, 2000). Case study permits the incorporation of an epistemological perspective that influences which questions are necessary for my investigation and interpretive frameworks to analyze findings (Collins, 2000; Merriam, 1998; Solórzano & Yosso, 2009; Yin, 2003). The primary phenomenon this study is concerned with is the incompletion rate of Black students in post-secondary educational institutions. My case study presents a collective study bound together through testimony, interviews, and counter story of the research participants. Each case focuses on the individual group's story organically created, interpreted, and thematically organized into a collaborative binding of experiences. Case study allows the counter story of Racially Stigmatized Identities to provide a tool for analysis and guidance to

78

the research to navigate through the issues related to the marginalized and oppressed populations (Smith-Maddox & Solórzano, 2002). Testimonial inquiries resulting from the collective cases are important because each individual case contains a cultural representation based in the experiences of each individual participant (Lockridge, 1988; Richardson, 1997). The collective case study method investigates in detail and through critical data collection the contexts of a particular phenomenon (Stake, 2000; Yin, 2003). The strength of a collective case study as opposed to a single case is the possibility of analyzing conclusions and the similarities across multiple differences in each case to develop a diverse discourse in the research findings (Yin, 2003).

Rationale for the Researcher's Theoretical Framework

Black feminist theory and critical race theory were selected as the theoretical lens to allow framing an inquiry to identify "the political choices and power driven ideologies and embedded forces that categorize, oppress, and exclude" (Marshall, 1997, p. 13). The coupling of Black feminism and critical race theory serve as primary theoretical frameworks within my case where I create a counter story drawn from the participants' testimonies that included institutional experiences with their race, class, and gender and sexuality and other intersectional subordinations (Delgado, 1995; Ladson-Billings, 2009).

Qualitative research studies conducted by Seidman (2006), Solórzano and Yosso (2009), and other researchers informed my research phenomenon simply because of the diverse cultural experiences their research participants brought, thus allowing me to create my initial understanding of the present research. For example, Astin (1968, 1971), Feagin and Sikes (1995), Fine (1991), and Hyman (1954) informed my research as their works offered the ability to openly engage participants through interviewing, incorporation of theoretical frameworks in relation to my study, testimony, and journaling; they also allowed the power of their participants' voices to organically create data. According to the theoretical constructs of critical race theory and Black feminism, I explored situational phenomena (Hancock & Algozzine, 2006; Merriam, 1998). For example, critical race theory encompasses four types of counter stories: the counter-narrative, personal stories, other people's stories, and composite stories (Delgado & Stefanic, 2001; Delgado, 1998; Solórzano & Yosso, 2009). In order to locate meaning in the counter stories, the researcher must be willing to practice theoretical sensitivity, which allows them to construct meaning through critical and ethnic theoretical frameworks (Bernal, 1998; Ladson-Billings, 2000; Strauss & Corbin, 1990). Counter stories and testimonies comprise data; they are ethnic epistemologies and racialized discourses in which the participant and the researcher are always subjects of knowledge (Delgado, 1998; Ladson-Billings, 2000). Moreover, critical race theory and Black feminism attribute importance to epistemological development and racialized discourses. Both theories acknowledge the intellectual ability of the knower, in my case, the research participants, Black students, and the theoretical frameworks support the

80

investigation of epistemological experiences that differ from a dominant perspective (Fine & Weis, 2010; Gildersleeve et al., 2003; Howard-Hamilton, 2003; Schwartz & Bower, 1997).

Carby (1985) addresses testimony as a particular form of dialogue, one that is an assertion of difference, especially involving a historical oppressive recollection. Recollection creates a space for a process of painful liberation. The testimony and historical document analysis in my research, which exist within the epistemological experiences of the participants, will serve as the justifying binding system for the participants' case (Stake, 2000; Yin, 2003). The integration of these experiences served as a force to analyze the phenomenological, axiological, epistemological, and ontological impacts of the agency (Holland et al., 1998; Wertsch, 1998).

Analyzing Case Study Through Theoretical Frameworks

Black feminism and critical race theory provide critical lenses to examine the incompletion rates among Blacks in post-secondary educational institutions and identify the numerous intersectional impacts through the use of the case study (Kursh, 2006; Marshall & Rossman, 2011; Merriam, 1998; Roach, 2007; Yin, 2003, 2004). This inquiry takes into account the institution's influence on Black students' graduation rates and the authorial value that may result from their experiences that can create a space for the foundation of knowledge to emerge (Ladson-Billings, 2000; Wynter, 1992).

My case studies used theoretical frameworks that included the situational impact that policies and procedures within these institutions have on Black students during their higher educational trajectories. Such frameworks provide a perspective that positions institutions as power holders and students, often, as victims that lead the intersectional influential dynamics that can affect post-secondary incompletion rates; this is known as the pushout (Fine, 1991) or the coercive discharge of Black students. Black feminism and critical race theory call for a research reinterpretation to counter the traditional paradigms of the discriminatory misrepresentation of Racially Stigmatized Identities that solidify institutional practices (Bell, 1992; Collins, 2000; Hernstein & Murray, 1996; Hooks, 1984; Hooks, 1992; Solórzano & Yosso, 2009). The questions within this proposed research critically investigated the experiences of Black students to gain an understanding of their experiences in institutions of higher education.

The following tenets of Black feminism and critical race theory have been merged together and will serve as the theoretical foundation for this study:

1. To challenge the dominant Eurocentric mainstream ideologies that provide the foundation of hegemonic elitist (Collins, 2000) structures of traditionally White[8] post-secondary educational institutions and their effect on the educational experiences of Black students (Collins, 2000; Delgado & Stefanic, 2001);

---

[8] Traditionally and in this study, White institutions are defined as post-secondary educational institutions the majority of whose faculty and student population identify as White/Caucasian.

2. The intercentricity of racism in education and its political influence on the educational institution and political structure that reinforces the oppression of Black students (Yosso, 2005; Collins, 2000; Fine, 1991);

3. The incorporation of counter storytelling as a research methodology that analyzes the historical and contemporary context of racial institutionalized discrimination in academic and social structures in post-secondary education that does not support Black students during their post-secondary educational pursuit (Bell, 1987, 1992; Delgado, 1995).

4. To explore and analyze the experiential knowledge and address and develop an alternative to socially constructed mainstream White privileged ideologies responsible for Black students not completing their 4–6-year bachelor degree programs. The theoretical frameworks of critical race theory and Black feminism have established an analytical tool that provides an explanation for the impact of race and humanness as property and how these intersections influence educational inequities (Beverly, 2000; Ladson-Billings, 2000; Ladson-Billings & Tate, 1995).

Research Questions

To examine the research tenets within the frameworks of critical race theory and Black feminism, the following research questions were formed:

1. What academic and social experiences do Black students face in post-secondary educational institutions that impact their graduation with a bachelor's degree?

Sub Questions

1. What social and academic interactions of Black students with the university's administration they feel has impacted their post-secondary educational experience?

2. What have been Black students' experiences regarding the curriculum[9] in college courses within the university that represent academic contexts that impacted their presence in those contexts?

3. What experiences did Black students encounter regarding academic and social support systems in or not in place at the university and how are such systems important influences on their degree program completion?

Final Question

4. How will multiple experiences of Black students in post-secondary education institutions transform institutional policies and procedures to help improve their graduation rates?

———————————————

Research Design: Data Collection Methods

Participant Sample and Site Description

The research was conducted at a four-year public Hispanic serving institution in the Southwestern region. Throughout the study, the institution is referred to by the pseudonym State College of the Southwest. Hispanics account for 44% of the student population, but the institution is predominantly White, precisely 47% (Institutional Research Planning and Outcome Assessment, 2010). The Black student population within this university is approximately 3% and Native Americans account for 2.7% of the population. The university has a population of over 18,000 students; 81% are enrolled full time. The university offers a number of bachelors, masters, and doctoral degree programs[10].

Due to the qualification criteria set for participants in my study, purposeful sampling was used. Patton (1990) noted that to understand a particular phenomenon, researchers must select a sample in which maximum information can be learned. LeCompte and Preissle (1993) stated that the criteria determined by the researcher in a purposeful sample forms a direct reflection of the purpose of the study. The experiences of Black students in post-secondary educational institutions form the primary focus in my case study (Merriam, 1998; Patton, 1990). For this study, nine participants were

---

[10] The number of degree plans offered by the university was not disclosed in order to prevent compromising the university in which the research will take place in any way.

divided into three groups: Group 1 included three students (currently enrolled in the university), Group 2 included three students who have already graduated from the university, and Group 3 included three pushouts from the university. The study took place over an eight-week timeframe. The qualitative data collection methods used were historical documentation analysis, focus group interviewing, observation, and journaling (Marshall & Rossman, 2011). I advertised the study through the department of Black programs; a flyer requesting participants who meet the criteria of the study was posted on their list serve and billboard. The flyer requested the contact information of local residents who are no longer attending school as well as those who had departed and left the institution. I posted a notice on the list serve every day until I had gathered all nine participants.

The participants required to fulfill the following criteria to be eligible for the study:

1. Members of Group 1 had to be enrolled at least half or full time at the institution at the time of the research;
2. Must identify racially as Black;
3. Flexible with regard to time so that they are available for meetings and interviews;
4. Enrolled in the university for at least one semester;
5. Three students who departed/were pushed out (who also met the criteria of 2–3, 7);

86

6. Three students who graduated with a bachelor's degree from the university, no longer enrolled or otherwise involved with the institution in any way (who also meet the requirements of 2–3);

7. Have regularly scheduled access to the internet and are willing to participate in online journaling and discussion.

    Participants were asked to email me with the following information that allowed them to identify themselves using the given descriptors or parameters: race, age, years of attendance, availability, and willingness to participate in focus groups and observational methods. This procedure assisted me in selecting the participants and scheduling the initial meeting and following interviews. The participants were required to fill out a consent form [see Appendix A] that informed them of the requirements of participating in journal writing. The participants also signed a form of confidentiality, because each interview was to be conducted in groups of three. The confidentiality form aimed to protect the privacy of each participant as well as the institution. All participants in the study needed to meet the researcher at scheduled times; they also had to be willing to an open interview about their experiences on campus. The flyer informed possible participants about the consent form and that no extrinsic rewards for participation would be offered. The first choice for the selection of students depended on physical location. If participants who satisfied the criteria of being graduates, current students, or pushouts were located in the city where the study was taking place, they were given priority over

87

those no longer in the physical area. Although this was not a determining factor in the end, it played a role in the selection process. The participants were informed of the purpose of the study through the consent form and were asked what pseudonym they desire to protect their confidentiality throughout the study. A majority of participants in the study were former mentees whom I worked with as a student advisor in the Department of Black programs at State College of the Southwest. Locating participants was not a challenge because of my familiarity with current and past students in the department.

Ensuring Participant Safety

Each participant was given an individual file labeled with their pseudonym and was further required to save their online journaling documentation under that pseudonym. The consent form also informed participants that they will be interviewed about their academic and social experiences within the institution. They were further told that I would inquire about any experiences on campus that informed their perceptions and interactions with faculty, other students, campus organizations, administrative happenings, and other issues on campus.

Focus Group Interviews and Procedures

Focus group interviewing was used in this study. The interview questions were the same for each group. The interviews and journals were semi-structured to maintain the participants' focus on the research questions regarding the purpose of the study. I asked the participants questions to initiate the interviews and journal writings, but

participants were encouraged to write and speak freely. I asked questions that required

the participants to reflect on particular events and situations within a particular context

[see Appendix F]. Focus group interviewing facilitated an informative interaction from

multiple perspectives and allowed both verbal and non-verbal communication.

Participants were sectioned off into the following three focus groups: participants

currently enrolled in the university, those who graduated from the university, and those

who were pushed out. I used focus group interviews to allow the participants to provide

oral testimony and written journaling of what implication their experiences in the

institution had on their academic journey. Qualitative focus group design is used to

illustrate the experiences of participants in greater detail. The purpose of the focus group

was to guide group discussion and share a generation of wealth that includes

participants' experiences and beliefs. Focus groups in qualitative research contribute

depth and meaning to the research process in my methodology (Marshall & Rossman,

2011). There were a total of nine focus groups meetings, one at the start of the research

(separately with each group), one two to three weeks into the research (separately with

each group), and a final meeting two weeks prior to the end of the study (separately with

each group).

Critical race theorists and Black feminism scholars highlighted the strengths of

case studies as follows: 1) exploring and discovering concepts that relate to the pushout rate of Black students; 2) adding context and depth to the understanding of the phenomenon; 3) providing the participants' interpretation of the phenomenon; 4) allowing the observation of participants' collective interaction (Fine, 1991; Solórzano et al., 2000). Focus group interviews create a space to listen, record and the opportunity to collaboratively share these experiences. Focus groups allow participants to forge a setting that enables the transfer of knowledge from participant to researcher (Bohm, 1985; Stake, 2000). Within this context of interviewing, there is a sharing of political, social, and cultural experiences and such experiences impel a realization, an atmosphere for the development of a counter story. Critical race theory and Black feminism provide a foundation that interprets this meaning in a cultural context. During the focus group, I videotaped, took notes, and used a digital recorder to gather information not initially apparent. Prior to recording the interview and turning on the video camera and digital recorder, each participant was reminded they needed to refer to each other by their pseudonyms to protect their identity. Each focus group interview lasted a minimum of 60 minutes and the maximum time allowed was 90 minutes. The focus group interviews were not expected to last longer than the set time of 60 minutes. As the researcher, I was willing to extend the time period due to the detailed descriptions and extent of openness naturally developed in the interview process by the participants. The last focus group interview was a summary and wrap up at the end of the semester for the participants to speak on their overall experience. Participation in the study was voluntary; participants were notified of the option to withdraw from the study at any time. The more I interacted with the participants and allowed them to see me, communicate with me, and freely express themselves, a deepening sense of trust emerged between the participant that may not have existed prior to the research (Marshall & Rossman, 2011; Stake, 1995, 2000).

Participant Journals

The purpose of the journal was to facilitate participant recollection and reflection process, to capture additional written personal experiences (Chase, 2010). One objective of the journal was to serve as a foundation if participants could not remember an incident initially; they could begin to take notes so they did not forget possible important details. Participants who attended the university also had the opportunity to carry journals with them to class and social events for the purpose of note taking if they encountered a situation. They could also share the information during the focus group interviews. Immediately before the interview, I made copies of each participant's journal entries, so that I did not need to hold on to their journals during my thematic coding process. A majority of the information in their journals consisted of answers to the research questions that I had sent via text message and email to each individual participant prior to the interviews. The journals also allowed me to perform consistent member check-ins and send them copies of their own words and prescriptions to ensure that I received correct information and did not misquote any of their responses.

Providing participants certain questions prior to the focus group allowed the participants time to reflect on their experiences and remember details before the stories were shared in group sessions. When we came together in the focus group, they began to share experiences with other participants; this helped them recall events during their testimonies as well as validate data within my study. Participants were allowed to retain their journals at the end of the study. As the researcher, I also kept my own hand-written journal as well as digital journal that I referred to multiple times throughout Chapter 5 to add detailed accounts to the counter story [see Chapter 5].

Observation

Observation played a small part in my study. It is a key method of investigation because it allows personal contact during activities and operations within the university for the researcher (Stake, 2000). The characterization of qualitative research requires researchers to reflect, reinterpret, and revise constantly in the creation of meaning (i.e., coding). In order to provide critical and adequate observations, as a researcher, I needed to recall observational experiences from past doctoral coursework that required rigorous and technical research methods (Patton, 1999). Courses such as quantitative and qualitative research (EDUC 576; EDUC 613), in-depth qualitative research methods (EDUC 606), and dissertation seminar and qualitative research (EDUC 694) required descriptive writing and careful preparation for field research. Reviewing the previous works, notes, and professorial critiques of my work completed during these courses helped hone my critical observational skills. Another step in the growth of my observational method was conducting meetings with experienced methodologists prior to and throughout the study to receive new knowledge, critique, and feedback pertaining to my research methods.

1. I shadowed the participants to social and academic events within the institutional context and documented their behaviors and interactions on charted field notes. These observational documentations included social, political, and/or cultural events hosted by different groups within the university [see Appendix D].

2. The field notes were formatted as follows: the observation of student interaction within the campus setting to include a variety of settings and meetings, shadowing individual students to class, observing their interactions with an array of campus staff, university entities, as well as peers [see Appendix D].

3. I recorded my observations through field notes as well as non-verbal and verbal interactions through an electronic tape recorder and digital camera set up in the room (Miles & Huberman, 1994). After each interview and observation, I recorded and wrote a verbal abstract of the observation. The recordings took place in a private location where I could openly speak into the recorder what I observed on the whole within the scenario, critical questions that I may want to ask the participants during the interview, and a summary/conclusion of the events that took place during the observation.

Understanding the cultural differences or similarities of the participants and the institution allows new experiential knowledge for me as the researcher which is critical to this study.

Observation provided scope for myself as the researcher to conduct an analysis of Black students as well as an opportunity for new vantage points to emerge to support my research data collection and analysis (Marshall & Rossman, 2011). The method also provided the opportunity to examine knowledge and note relationships of the intersections of race and education that impact the knowledge participants brought to the study. Observation unveiled the opportunity to engage in the social and academic culture of the participants as well as their interpretation of the institution's actions. Highwater (1981) stated "the greatest distance between people is not space but culture" (p. 3) (Ladson-Billings, 2000). This statement, as cited by Highwater, is relevant as it explains the need for observation to explore the participants' culture, dialogical spaces, and the perspectives of those no longer in the university setting. Participants were asked to submit a monthly schedule of events that I was open to attend prior to the observation. The consent form explained the types of observational data to be collected for the study [see Appendix A].

Crystallization of the Research Data

Trustworthiness was established through the method of crystallization. The data in this study was validated through the crystallization of field notes, observation, journaling, interviewing, and historical documentation analysis. Due to the multiple data collection methods involved, crystallization was a primary choice because it provided a naturalistic outcome related to the communication and experiences of the research participants (Janesick, 2000). One objective of my research was to gain experiential knowledge from students within a particular setting and utilize that knowledge to deconstruct the pushout phenomenon of Black students. This method connected to critical race theory and Black feminism because they seek the counter story of Racially Stigmatized Identities to construct meaning from intersectional experiences. Both theories legitimize the experiences of marginalized, oppressed groups on the basis of known and unknown institutional isms. Since my research focuses primarily on the intersection of race and education, areas in which both theories have a strong foundation of research, this was suitable to explore the political, social, and cultural phenomena of the world of Black students, especially within educational institutions. The method of crystallization enhanced the theoretical perspectives and enabled data analysis by providing a deepened, complex, thoroughly partial understanding of my research topic (Janesick, 2000, p. 392). Janesick described the epistemological approach by providing new and overlooked knowledge regarding how the world works and critically analyzes the construction of meaning for groups facing discrimination based on intersectional differences (Lincoln & Guba, 1985).

The social world experiences that influence my research participants' life were recognized in the facets of crystallization and enhanced through the theoretical frameworks of Black feminism and CRT. A descriptive understanding through participant testimony addressing the effect of students in marginalized positions within education, created by the institution, emerged over time as the data was crystallized. The depth, richness, and possibility provided by the responses and data collected through the participants' stories expanded, changed, and altered the findings, just like the formation of a crystal.

Member check-ins helped validate my research findings. Checking with members and allowing them to review the information as the themes emerged enabled me to remain as true as possible to the participants' voices. The analyses of research findings incorporated first-person perspective and included voice through quotes that fit into themes copied verbatim from the research data.

For conducting every focus group interview, I used a digital recorder and camera. The data resulting from each interview was transcribed verbatim and was collected through multiple sources and forms of data collection during a prolonged engagement process which included multiple reviews of the data collected and conducted at the end of the study. The university's Learning Resource Center provided the technological equipment I needed to store the focus group interviews in mp3 format on a password protected USB drive and laptop. In addition to my notes, I also possessed electronic documentation of the data for analyses as well. Interviews were transcribed verbatim, and because of the number of interviews, the transcriptions were made by a professional transcriber. The paid transcriber also signed a letter of confidentiality [see Appendix B]. All interviews were assigned by the date of the interview and coded according to the atmosphere and code names of participants. I also developed an audit trail to maintain consistency and accuracy of the data collected during my study. The camera did not only record video also but the voice of the participants, because I decided to use the data during the writing of the counter story; the participants had the option to protect their identity and did not have to worry about confidentiality.

Data Analysis

Coding for Themes

In developing the thematic sections of my research, each individual case not only provided diverse perspectives in the same context but also, due to the method of crystallization, created an opportunity which allowed the emergence of themes from the counter narrative of Black students through both a critical race theory and Black feminist lens.

I took the notes from my observations and research and relied on them to allow the emergence of themes that developed throughout my study. This process involved multiple reviewing of audio and video interviews, observational note taking, reviewing transcriptions, and journal writings. During the initial review, I did not construct any

97

themes. I randomly placed notes from the interviews and literature on the post-it wall. I further let the data crystallize through a repetitive and intense review process (Marshall & Rossman, 2011). This process involved the repetitive viewing of transcriptions and digital voice recordings privately and granted the time to critically evaluate the testimonies and journals of my participants through the theoretical frameworks.

I organized the data according to the date and time of the interviews and stored the information locked in a safe. This step was crucial, especially during the data analysis process, due to the fact that it organized the information and made it easily accessible. Each individual participant developed their own pseudonym that verified who they were, for the purpose of confidentiality and personalization to the participants during the interview process. I knew my responsibility as a researcher was to protect my human subjects and that I had to remain tediously cautious and take the adequate steps to ensure their safety and confidentiality. I had a total of nine participants, and in order to keep track of all the data they provided, I had to review it and organize it daily. By reviewing each transcription and journal writing word for word and line by line, the context allowed the themes to emerge. I was constantly reviewing the interviews, my notes, critical race theory and Black feminist literature, and the journal writings of participants. I allowed myself two to three weeks between each interview, a manageable amount of time, to become organized and start to construct and organize my themes on a daily basis.

The Emergence of Busara the Alter Ego during Crystallization

During the crystallization process, I developed a dissertation wall to allow the emergence of themes to crystallize. The wall was a 9 x 10 foot space divided into four large sheets of paper that evenly covered the wall [see Appendix E]. Each sheet consisted of color-coded post-its from transcription highlights and journal entries from each group, literary findings from previous studies, possible themes, and my own reflections and journal highlights. During this phase of crystallization, I was able to build on the tenets of the study and themes that emerged. I also reflected on critical race theory and the method of counter storytelling to transform the data into an actual counter story.

I highlighted multiple tenets of critical race theory and combined them with Black feminism and thus an alter ego was created by the name of Busara. Busara is formally introduced in Chapter 5; he was also inspired by previous works such as Derrick Bell's Geneva Crenshaw in the book *And We Are Not Saved* (1987) and Richard Delgado's Rodrigo Crenshaw from *The Rodrigo Chronicles* (1995); both alter egos were created to reinforce the theoretical frameworks of critical race theory and engage in critical discussions of race and racism in education in multiple facets. As I analyzed the data, I realized that in order to remain honest to counter storytelling as a research method, it was crucial that I encompass the scholarly structure of counter storytelling, which makes it such a fascinating methodology.

Interview Organization

Each file was stored alphabetically in a locked file cabinet. The DVDs along with the digital tapes were also stored in the locked file cabinet. I consistently reviewed each DVD before the next interview to observe possible changes in body language and emotions and expressions of participants that I may have overlooked or possibly misinterpreted during our face-to-face meetings. At the beginning of each group meeting, I addressed this with individual participants to ensure I had correctly interpreted their actions. I reaffirmed their actions, to stay true to their words, but also because I knew that I wanted to incorporate as much depth as possible within my counter story.

Document Analysis

In my data collection methods, I discussed self-reflection. I believe that a major part of this process surfaced as I immersed myself in the data. I analyzed and reanalyzed the data repeatedly and then wrote in my own journal about the mental processes I was undergoing as a researcher to maintain a clear and critical understanding of my self-growth throughout this research process (Villenas, 2010). The continual examination of my research through my life experiences is a quality of good workmanship that helped define my craftsmanship (Mills, 2010). The data collected in the interviews was shared with the participants throughout the interviews and in the final debriefing. The data from this process will not be destroyed and will be kept in my possession for no more than five years and then destroyed; I am planning to use the information in future writings and for publishing purposes.

Role and Position of the Researcher

As the researcher, I served as the arbiter, integrator, and the final narrator of the cultural discourse presented in the final data collected during my study (Chase, 2010; Gergen & Gergen, 2000; Ladson-Billings, 2000). This research might be controversial yet is critical for setting a direction that will prompt contemplation (Marshall & Rossman, 2011). In the course of this research, I went through multiple processes of self-reflection, due to my position and privilege in comparison to the participants. I took steps to reprogram my consciousness to not only reflect on previous formal and informal educational practices, curriculum, and policies but also to creatively and critically embrace my cultural traditions into my everyday teachings, research purpose, and praxis (Freire, 1970; Pinar, 1992; Bell et al., 1990). I continuously critiqued the origins of my questions, motives, emotional stability, and experiences during data collection. I believe that certain findings stirred up emotions and memories, and in order to deal with that process, I needed to read and analyze the research literature and regularly schedule meetings with my committee, advisor, and my colleagues. I had to develop a support system that incorporated openness and allowed redirection and clarity as required. There were times when I became overwhelmed by the participants' testimonies and had to step away from the data analysis to regain focus. I also had to constantly read and review multiple readings within the literature to gain a clear understanding the research process. Awareness about other researchers and sharing of experiences assisted me in admitting my own perspective, assumptions, and sensitivities. I created an open space to re-analyze my own thoughts and expressions; the process of maintaining a personal written journal was extremely beneficial during this process. I was mentally preparing for such moments, especially during interviews when I wanted desperately to share my experiences with my participants. However, I had to be mindful of objectivity and thus remained disciplined by enforcing the notion that the research was not about my testimony.

My perspective shaped the research and now I had to humble myself and let the acquisition of new knowledge assume a prominent presence within my research process. At the same time, I was aware that this placed me in a sensitive position as a researcher, because I had to be careful to not to let this heavily influence my research practice, methods, and outcomes. Through reflection and during certain times of the research process, I recalled multiple encounters with sexism, racism, and classism in my educational pursuit. When this happened, I created steps to engage in reflexivity by writing and critical reflection of my own thoughts to use these experiences to reexamine various discourses that potentially affected the research outcome (Collins, 2000; Lutrell, 2010; Mills, 2010; Villenas, 2010). In order to provide a trustworthy research study, I incorporated processes of multiple interviews, observation, transcription, participant journals, and coding crucial to the formulation of organized and adequate record keeping, true to the voice of each participant (Anfara & Mertz, 2006; Lutrell, 2009; Marshall & Rossman, 2011; Spradley, 1979).

I wanted to ensure that I remained true to my participants and their words. I constantly read other studies similar to my research approach to gain new insight and support from researchers who faced similar challenges. As a member of a marginalized and privileged community, I have inherited the obligation to consider how the research will impact not only my life but also the participants' and the phenomenon as a whole (Villenas, 2009). I occupy a position of privilege. Another process that I undertook to address the potential interruption of my bias within my research was to attend regularly scheduled meetings with my advisor and my doctoral committee, especially my methodologist. I engaged in open and critical dialogue with these scholars who performed similar research. Listening to alternative perspectives and getting second, third, and fourth opinions was highly beneficial to me as a scholar in the making and my research.

Ethical Considerations

The participants in this study were treated in compliance with the ethical guidelines of the American Psychological Association and the Institutional Review Board of the university for which I am researching (IRB). In the event of any emotional distress placed upon any participant during the study, they were directed to the free services provided by the university counseling center located on campus and one within the city for non-students. The major risks within this study were protecting the participants' identity as well as any staff or faculty whose names were mentioned during the interviewing, journaling, and observation process. Each person's identity was protected through the steps listed in the data collection and analysis phase of the methods section. At no time did the researcher risk the academic or professional career of any characters in the participants' testimonies or the participants themselves. Participants were also informed that they could withdraw from the study at any time if necessary (see Appendix A).

Conclusion

Chapter 3 offered a description of my research methods and design. I lent insight into my rationality, philosophies, and the theories that inform my study. The data analysis methods and critical processes I experienced as the researcher were detailed. In this chapter, I incorporated the theoretical frameworks of my study and their role in my research methods to supplement perspective, clarity, and comprehend the data I planned to collect. I explained my role and position as the researcher and the reflective processes I undertook throughout the study. I explained the purpose of crystallization to code my themes and ethical considerations of the study. I also explained the safety measures, right adherence, and respect I practiced towards my participants.

Chapter IV

Case Studies

Introduction

Case studies have been presented from a first person perspective to describe each individual participant's experience, although they are grouped as collective cases. Under each pseudonym, a quote representing each participant has been placed, which precedes their testimony. The profile of each participant includes a personalized testimony of their educational journey. The participants were asked to select a quote that represented their voice and their educational trajectory. The closing section of each profile presents a tribute to their educational aspirations. The educational aspirations were placed at the end of the profiles to provide a better understanding of the participants before advancing to Chapter 5.

Coady (1973) explained that a testimony is by nature a reliable form of evidence, because it provides a perspective concerning the world's reality (Graham, 2000). As the primary researcher, I incorporated testimonies to communicate each participant's world of personal and academic experiences. The incorporation of participant background in this chapter offers insight into multiple experiences that manifest within the educational trajectory of each participant.

Denzin and Lincoln (2013) labeled the qualitative researcher a bricoleur, one who assembles images and montages[11]. The bricoleur in this chapter was interpretive. Each profile was constructed through the method of testimony and quilted according to the background of each participant. The incorporation of participant background was cycled into the story to add a brief sense of complexity to the viewer's construction of the interpretation of the participants as the counter story unfolds in Chapter 5. Data collected throughout this study set the tone for creating a montage to inform administrative policies and procedures within the institution.

The data collected from the participants' profiles was limited to their testimonies, journal writings, and two interview sessions. The interviews were divided into two sessions. The first interview aimed to ascertain personal information regarding the racial climate of the campus in relation to the participants' experiences (including interactions with faculty, staff, and administration). The second interview was focused on the personal background information and any additional experiences, from the post-secondary educational trajectory and aspirations of each participant.

As elucidated in Chapter 3, the case study method was adopted "it allows the counter story of Racially Stigmatized Identities to provide a tool for analysis and guidance to the research to navigate through the issues that relate to the marginalization,

---

[11] Lincoln and Denzin (2013) described a montage as a method of editing cinematic images to create a picture. Montaging was practiced by the researcher during the data analysis process. In this study, the picture being painted of each participant is their profile.

silencing, and oppression of those populations" (Smith-Maddox & Solórzano, 2002). In this research investigation, the case study method allowed the researcher to examine in "real life context" (Yin, 1994) the occurrences shared through the participant's stories.

The formulization of each question was designed to provide a foundation of critical analysis for each participant to reflect and engage in dialogue. The dialogical space provided each participant the opportunity to share with the researcher, as well as other participants, their experiences in post-secondary education. While presenting the cases in this chapter, I tried my best to include the participant's authentic words and journal reflections while interpolating my own journal experiences, which I recorded following each interview and observation.

Every participant in the study played a vital role in the creation of this chapter. To promote the authenticity of the wording used by each participant, I used the member check in process during the second interview and final debriefing. Stake (2000) suggested that a critical component in ensuring the accuracy of research is allowing participants to review a draft of one's chapter and permit the opportunity to raise objections regarding the interpretation of their words.

The Pushouts

Polo

> *Stumbling is not falling.*
> Malcolm X

Excuses are abuse to your potential.
Polo

Background

I would like to introduce myself as Polo. My identity is a 21-year-old Back male.

I am from Compton, California. As a child, I always had to share because there

was two of me. April 14, 1992 my mother gave birth to two twin boys. Polo and

Gap, we were so much alike as babies, from helping each other climb out the

crib to crying together, even our cry was in sync. As we grew up, we totally went

two separate ways. Gap learned how to live the street life and be a young man,

while I, Polo went the other and dealt with finding myself and accepting the fact

that I could be different. This is where, like, my educational journey begins. Kids

are so harsh, so rude, and sometimes kids can be kind, patient, but kids are so

blunt. As a child, I was constantly picked on; this situation was unavoidable

because of my personality. My girl cousins completely outnumber my boy

cousins. My twin and I grew up around a majority of young girls. I was more

drawn to the activities of the girls; I picked up on some their habits, like jumping

rope. Due to the decisions I made as a young child, kids called me gay and I was

picked on, I was beat up and this dragged my brother into the situation because

he was my twin. I did not become very socially active throughout elementary

and middle school. I didn't go on field trips, I would visit another class. I stayed in class for lunch. My education at one point had become so stressful I tested to receive home schooling, because I was afraid to go to school.

Due to the bullying I encountered, I began to just focus on school. My grades became my priority; I was an all A student and always made the honor roll. I was never late to class; I never missed a day of class in four years of high school. Throughout elementary, I never received a failing grade – no satisfactory, I was always good or excellent. The type of mentality I had I believed I could pass all my classes in one week and not have to go to school anymore. I could just, like, the Disney Channel character Smart Guy. He was somebody I looked up to as a young child. I wanted to be like him and just ace every class and not have to attend school. I was the kid that was just picked on; I didn't know how to fight back, so my twin brother did most of my fighting. I was afraid of junior high, but I was ready, I was ready to take on the challenge. During this transition, my mother encouraged me; she was very supportive. She always acknowledged that I was different; she would explain that I was too young to know what I actually wanted out of life. I will never forget the day my dad caught me playing with a Barbie doll and he beat me bloody; my grandma called the police, and Child Protective Services filed a case against my dad for child abuse. From that moment in my life, I really faced various social issues that would and have continued to affect my performance in school.

My sophomore year in high school I experienced another traumatic event. My mother's boyfriend was very abusive; he abused my twin brother and I, as well as my mother. The situation had arrived at a point where my brother and I could no longer take the beatings. We began to fight back and then the next thing I remember was my mom handing us a bag with all of our clothes inside and slamming the door in our face. Gap and I lived in Helen Keller Park on El Segundo Boulevard and Vermont Avenue for a whole 3 weeks before anyone was notified, even our teachers. I caught the train to school every morning. I had to wake up early enough to get to Compton, because the train didn't run pass my location off the streets of Pilmer and Wellmington. I would take a shower at my best friend's house. My best friend Shawna (Pseudonym) and her dad would get vouchers for me from the school. They informed me that I could not live in their house, but I had the opportunity to take showers; they already had a lot of kids living in the home. Through all the hardships, I still managed to keep a 3.83 G.P.A, but I remember my twin brother dropping out of school. I tried to encourage him by telling him we can still do this, we can still make it in life. In the end, Gap felt like we didn't have enough support and he just gave up on school. When he gave up, I began to give up, like my grades started falling, and I stopped going to school – I ran from education. Prior to this, I never ran from

110

something in my life. I developed the habit of running, and till this day, I am still trying to break free from that habit.

Part of the reason why I left this institution was due to my running away and not putting up a fight when I encountered trials and tribulations. I was not strong enough for the challenge at that time but eventually had to overcome the situation. My education is important to me because it involves growth and development. Also, it's a way of life. You're always going to be educating people in many different forms. Education is always present, whether it's teaching someone how to tie a shoe, teaching someone something in your field, or just educating your mom or someone on how to operate a new type of technology. You should always be willing to be educated. Education is the way of life. (Interview, April 2, 2013)

Educational Aspirations

I feel like my education is my voice, it's my stamp, of me being independent, me being responsible, being the first step of me accomplishing my dreams and my goals. I will use this education that I receive to be the voice for other children that are scared to come out of the closet. I want to serve as a representative for children that have been abused, children that don't have support. I am going to encourage children that are still struggling to find themselves, whether it be a personality or someone that is trying to find their voice or someone that's trying to find their art or their craft. I want to be that voice for children. We need education in everything that we do and in every career you enter. You're going to have to educate your secretary how to answer a phone or your janitor how to clean a window. Educating someone is very important; it is a permanent part of the world. I'm going to use my education to give back to those who don't have help or don't have a voice. (Interview, April 2, 2013)

Danie

The road of life twists and turns and no two directions are ever the same. Yet our lessons come from the journey, not the destination.
Don Williams Jr.

Background

My name is Danie. I have spent most of my life being raised in Long Beach, California. I am a 26-year-old Black woman. The reason why I'm embarking on my education is because when I was growing up, I went through many hardships. I'm still young, but in my young life, I know that I can't get very far without a college education. I've been married and I've attended multiple community colleges. I have money issues, personal family issues, and I am currently at a very low point in my life. As contradictory as it sounds, I am also living some of the happiest points in my life, because I'm finally at a point where I'm just succeeding by deciding to continue my education. I enrolled at this institution I left and I fought to return, and I am on the right track to finally finishing my degree. I'm pushing myself to succeed and I do not have a large support system. Due to the hurdles I was experiencing academically and personally, I have learned a lesson from every one of those hurdles and I have fought tooth and nail to come back to school. I made up my mind that if I come back this time I really have to finish and not give up. Everything that I've done in my life I feel like I have never completed. There was many times when I would fall hard, but this time no matter what, I'm going to finish school. Throughout my entire life, especially in high school, I was heavily involved in sports and I didn't have to worry about other things because I was excelling in track and field. Through athletics, I was provided the opportunity to travel, which was something different. Traveling created a distance from my parents and I. My family and I never really had the chance to really build a strong relationship when I was growing up, even when I was in elementary. I can recall having issues with my elementary school teachers and my parents never taking my side or ever standing up for me, even if I did nothing wrong. Therefore, we never really established a relationship, not a very close one like they have with my brother and my sister. I feel as if I grew up on my own. Life was kind of hard because of the lack of guidance I had in my life. When I became a mother to my daughter, I didn't really understand what it meant to be a parent. I had no one mentoring me, nobody that wanted to take me under their wing, and explain to me what growing into my adulthood meant. My driving and inspiring force throughout my life have always been my two best friends and my little girl. I feel as if people have no idea what Black students at this institution have been enduring. I know that no matter what, at the end of the day, I'm going to have my education to fall back on, so I continue to fight for my degree. Therefore I need education – education is important to me because you need it to advance, to create a better life. (Interview, April 2, 2013)

Educational Aspirations

Having my education is giving me credit, and it's also inspiring. You can inspire someone to want to do better for themselves just by having an education. You can speak to people about the importance of education. I feel that we can use education to protect ourselves from what our government is trying to take from us. If you have one thing that you can give yourself in your life, it's your education, because you can obtain so much with an education whether you a bum on the street or you're in the White House. I would like to inspire anyone who is willing to listen to what I have to say. I want to spark their fire. I want to provide the motivation to give them that drive. I want to inspire people to have the attitude that they can do it, they can accomplish completing their education. I hear so many people, all the time who talk about how their struggles and challenges prevent them from pursuing their education. You hear people say "I went through this or I went through that" and I understand their struggle. It's so hard to truly understand where that person's coming from, if you've never walked in their shoes. Unless you just go through that situation yourself, so you can speak all you want, but you have to have something to back up your story. I want to empower other people, to give back and motivate others through my education. (Interview, April 2, 2013)

Unknown

Stay true to you.
Unknown

Background

My name is Unknown. I was born and raised in Compton, California. I consider myself a 22 year old Black male. Life for me was not too complicated. My educational journey was regular; I can't really remember a lot of details. I can't remember myself as a kid. I was just going to school. I can remember taking Spanish in 2nd grade, and my Spanish teacher was always very nice to me. I had a pretty regular education. I was the kind of person that was always to myself, always by myself. I didn't always agree with the actions of other people my age in my life. I didn't participate in the things that other children around me were involved in, activities such as smoking or drinking. I remember a lot of my peers would like to fight and they would just to jump other children my age. I never thought that was fair, so I stayed away from that part of my reality because of the negativity. I really didn't hang around too many people throughout school. I remember having a couple of friends but I also had many associates.

I wouldn't say my family and I suffered many struggles. I grew up with my intermediate family which is made up of my brothers and both my parents. I really enjoy the company of my family. I have never been a stranger to responsibility. I remember watching over and taking care of many of my little cousins. I was always the more responsible child; my parents would always place me in charge of taking care of my younger siblings and cousins. After spending so much time in California, I wanted something different in my life. I was ready to live on my own; ready to be me, ready to start my life. I was tired of sitting around doing nothing; I wanted to find out why I was put on this Earth. I knew at this time I needed something different in my life. I was ready for a change. I worked in California, I went to school in California, and it was as if I just merely existed. I knew that at that time I was ready to experience something else, something more challenging. Job Core in San Diego was originally my first choice after I completed high school. One day, I met TEN, a recruiter from the office of admissions; he talked me into trying out college, that's how I ended up down here in the southwest. I received an offer from this institution. You know, I already had friends who were enrolled in TEN's mentoring program and explained it was a good opportunity. I then decided to further my education. Education is important because knowledge is power. It's never a bad thing to have too much knowledge. (Interview, April 2, 2013)

Educational Aspirations

I use my education as a representation of my freedom. I say my freedom because I'm a free person, I'm a free spirit and want to show my freedom so others can gain their freedom. I really want to show other people like me that it is possible to gain a voice. I won't ever be scared to speak on anything that I disagree or agree with, my voice matters. I just want to be free. I think that everybody should be free to be who they are, and not let anybody, whether it's a friend, a relative, or an enemy to influence them to not be true to themselves. I feel that fear limits freedom; people are always scared. I just want to give off that vibe that people should always be true to themselves. (Interview, April 2, 2013)

Currently Enrolled Students

Cherise

> What doesn't kill you makes you stronger.
> Friedrich Nietzsche

Background

My name is Cherise, and I was born and raised in Los Angeles, California. I am a 23-year-old Black woman. I really remember my educational journey really starting in my senior year of high school. I went to high school in Long Beach,

California, Jordan High School. I had an awesome advisor, which I did take advantage of until my senior year of high school. My advisor's name was Ms. Layla (pseudonym), and she was assigned to be my advisor sophomore year in high school. I must say she was very helpful at all times. I could go visit her anytime of the day and she was available most of the time. Ms. Layla enrolled me into courses that she knew I would need in order to attend Cal State University in California. I wasn't really interested in going to college because I didn't have support coming from anywhere else besides her office. I wasn't living with my mom, and my dad was in prison. I lived with my aunt and grandmother. I was focused on graduating from high school because I wanted to do it for my parents and also for my siblings because I'm the oldest child. I was determined to set a goal–a good example for my one brother and three sisters. Ms. Layla reminded me that I was a decent student; according to my transcript, I never received below a C average throughout high school. I never repeated a class nor did I go to summer school to take up any additional classes. From that moment on, I look forward to completing college applications and I also began to take my future seriously. I can honestly say that Ms. Layla, my advisor, is the person that motivated me to attend college.

After I saw all the work she was doing for me I started to help myself. I registered to take my SAT and ACT which are college entrance/placement exams. I was accepted to Cal State Domingas Hills which is located in Carson, California. I went there for a semester, and then after that, I ended up at El Camino College in Torrance, California. I can honestly say that I was not taking full advantage of the opportunity to go to school to better myself and future. I went there for a few semesters on and off until I decided I wanted to go through a nursing program. So I took a semester from a community college and I went through a CNA program that I qualified for at the Goodwill in Long Beach, California. While I was completing the nursing program, I ran into an opportunity to go out of state and attend this university. Being on my own is just something that goes along with my character and personality; at that time in my life I feel like I was doing very bad and I desperately wanted to change that around. Although I kept my mind focused on the nursing program, I also focused on going to school out of state. I wanted to take advantage of the opportunity to go back to school and finish what I started. I still wanted to chase my goal and earn a bachelor's degree. I did achieve a few things, like receiving my CAN degree, but I felt like it just wasn't enough. On top of all of that, living in California was wearing me down. I was all for going out of state school and ready to take care of my future. I knew if I wanted to achieve a successful future, it required taking my education a lot more seriously. (Interview, April 2, 2013)

Educational Aspirations

I came here to college to finish what I started. I am going after my dreams, to set a positive example for my siblings, to do something that I knew I could do and lastly to get my college education, which will help my future to look bright. I believe education is important because it plays a major role in my future as far as, like, career, career choice, wisdom, knowledge. I want to go back to high schools and talk to students about college and try to get them to do the applications and fulfill other requirements it will take to get them to go out there. I know some people that did get involved back in California, but at the time I was in high school, I can't recall anyone doing that for our class. I know someone that went to this university and some people that still attend. Encouraging students to come to college to get the education is something we need more of in our communities. I can go on college tours or maybe even become a speaker at a high school. I can see myself as a mentor in the area of my major, which is business. I'm not exactly sure where I want to go in that but somewhere down the line maybe I can help. I see myself doing volunteer work or something along those lines to guide kids that are from my community. I wish that was done to me, like, I wish a lot of different stuff was said to me, preached to me, like, so that I could have been in a better position now. (Interview, April 2, 2013)

Renee

> *If you focus on results you will never change,*
> *but if you focus on change you will get results.*
> Jack Dixon

Background

My name is Renee. I'm 20 years of age and I was born and raised in Tucson,

Arizona. I am a strong, Black woman. I have been in private schools all

throughout my education except one year. I started my education in El Paso until

after my first year when I relocated to Tucson, Arizona. I didn't start to realize or

even understand the lack of diversity in private schools. Throughout 2nd – 7th

grade, I was the only Black child who attended the school. The first private

school I attended in Arizona was St. John's, the evangelist, catholic school,

which had grades pre-k through 8th. Most of the students, if not all, were

Mexican and more than a few spoke very little English. At one point I could

completely comprehend Spanish because of my surroundings. I didn't

understand the discrimination in how they were treating me while attending that

school. I was sent home when my mom had put braids in my hair because they

said it was a sign of gang violence. That action on behalf of the school was

corrected rapidly by my dad. I was told by art teachers that my work was ugly

and they always made me start over. I had been in many fights because one thing

my dad told me was not to let anybody hit me without hitting them back and

121

stick up for myself. I was picked on and stereotyped to where I punched a girl in her face and then sat in the office and got in trouble, but she went unpunished; and the list goes on. When I transferred from a Texas school to one in Arizona, my level of education was so much higher than my classmates. Many other kids in the second grade were still unable to read. In Texas, they put us on words of phonics in kindergarten, so it frustrated some teachers because they wanted to challenge. They put up with it until the 3rd grade until they decided my level was too high and moved me to the 5th grade. Throughout this time, my parents did their best to make the transition of moving, easier for me. My mom was involved with every school activity and field trip.

My mother made so many improvements and put so much money in the school to make it a family environment. For example, she set up morning and afternoon programs so that children were not left wandering around campus while waiting for parents. She set up volunteering for parents to drive to field trips, rather than us getting on city buses for our destination, and she set up carnivals to have on campus to get the community involved. My dad set up a girls' basketball team for the fourth graders and up and coached for free. After all that was done, a teacher that I already had once wanted me to stay in her class and gave the excuse that I was slow. This teacher wanted my mom to stay in her classroom. My mom refused and pulled me from the school in the middle of my 7thgrade year. My mom was going to enroll me in a public middle school for the 7th grade. When we got to the Tortelita middle school, they called my old school, and they lied and said I never finish the 6thgrade. So I had to repeat the 6th grade.

I was so excited for public school – no uniforms. My parents didn't want me just to pass through school; they wanted me to reach my full potential. So once 7thand 8th grade were over, I was right back at private school. I enjoyed private school. My teachers were actually interested in my success. If I was getting behind, they made sure I got back up to par; they would not allow me to fail and encourage me to never give up. I attended South Point Catholic College preparatory high school. In order to qualify for this institution, you must receive an above average on the entrance exam. Freshman year, our teachers were informing us we needed to start our academics strong in order to prepare for college. The classes were rigorous as well as the grading scale. Receiving a letter grade of an A was a 93 to a 100 and a B was an 85–92. Those are the only ones I'll mention because those were the only grades I was allowed to bring home. I finished high school with a 3.7 GPA and graduated with honors. I was a part of the national society of high school scholars, part of the student council, basketball team, immunity club, student athletic trainers, and the bicycle club. I was a busybody and still maintained my grades. I knew I was going to college; since middle school it's been drilled into me and I had no other choice. When I first started applying to schools I wanted to go to Emory College in Georgia or Purdue, but of course my overprotective mother did not allow it; she shot me and my dream down. Schools of that nature were too far and too expensive. When I received my letters back from the schools that I had applied to, I was accepted to every single one. You can imagine my frustration, so I had to narrow it down. One institution was a definite no because that area would get way too much snow, another was too far and my dad said I couldn't take my car. This institution won by default. Throughout my schooling, my parents only accepted the best out of me – A's and B's were the only thing deemed acceptable. They felt school associated activities were the only things I should have time for. To make matters worse, my curfew was when it got dark outside; I had to be in the house, no excuse. I thought they did this to be mean, but I've realized I'm truly blessed to have my parents put so much money and time into my education to ensure my success. My parents did not have it easy and did not want their children to go through the same struggle. (Interview, April 2, 2013)

Educational Aspirations

Receiving my college education is important because I need it to be successful. I want to be comfortable; I do not want any kind of financial struggles. I just want

124

to continue to live comfortably as I did, growing up. I don't know anything else. It's hard to think of a future goal right now. I'm just trying to finish school. My goal for after graduating, I think I'll work with families and inform them of what I went through while attending college. I was literally failing, an F student, on the verge of getting kicked out of school. I want to send the message to children that you can still graduate, you can still go back. There's no reason one failure should stop you from achieving your goals. I want to inform them that they can still go back to school. (Interview, April 2, 2013)

Gilbert

> *If you knock on doors and no one answers, build your*
> *Own door of success knock, open, and leap through.*
> B. L. Brown

Background

My name is Gilbert and I am 20 years of age. I was born in Bridgeport, Connecticut. My mom was attending and putting my dad through nursing school when she became pregnant and had to drop out. I was the first born child. I'm currently a sophomore junior, in college here at the university. My family is originally from Ghana, West Africa. My aunts and uncles all moved to either London or New York, so when I was born, she sent me to go live with my aunt. I have one sister and two younger brothers, and they've all lived over in London. My grandmother actually took me to London when I was two months old. I grew

125

up in Peckham, London until I was 6 years of age. My parents flew in frequently, once a year or once every two years. I didn't really know who my parents were till I was about six or seven years old, when I moved back to the United States. I have two brothers and one sister. When I came back, we all lived in a two-bedroom apartment in West Haven, Connecticut. At that time, things were tough for our family. My dad was still in school; he had to take his time because he drove trucks; he was a taxi cab driver; he's built homes, and he has worked many different odd jobs. My parents really struggled to provide for their kids. My family's struggle was my motivation once I got into high school.

I was bad in high school; I got into a lot of trouble. My parents always fought and argued. My dad got his RN, we moved out of there into another apartment and then we stayed there for a year while they looked for another home because we actually got evicted out of our old apartment. The eviction was rendered because my younger brothers came over and they were still young, like 5 and 6, and there were six of us sleeping in a two-bedroom apartment. My younger brothers always wanted to play and they would make noise. I have a lot of half siblings all on my dad's side. I have two older half-sisters, as well as a half brother that is born in December, so he's only a couple of years younger than me. My brother is a sophomore/junior at Penn State, so I have a lot of competition. My family started to do much better. We finally found an

126

affordable four-bedroom house out in the suburbs and my dad started making decent money and providing for his family. My mom started going back to school and working at the same time. I was in high school at the time and was getting into a lot of trouble. I liked to fight, I never tried gangs or drugs or anything of that nature. I was always suspended, always in trouble. I was expelled twice from high school. I needed 14 credits so I did school full time; I was also assigned to do community service to get extra credit. I played football, basketball, and I did night school, all to graduate on time and walk with my class. My mother would always tell me that I had to change my life.

I started college back home at a local community college because I graduated with a really miserable GPA but I still made it out of high school on time. Once I enrolled in college, my freshman year, I saw my GPA. I graduated with like a 1–1.9, from high school, and I thought to myself, damn, I barely graduated. I realized at this time that I had pulled it off. I wanted to be different than my peers. I knew that at least 60–65% of my graduating class either dropped out of college or moved back home. Many of them are working local jobs like Wendy's, McDonald's, and tanning salons. I turned it around in community college and earned my certified nursing assistant degree and a 3.3 GPA. I knew at this time that I had to leave home; I was ready to get out of the house. I don't really have any family out here but my mom has a really close friend, family friend, that lives out here and I wanted to go far, as far away from home as possible. There is a large amount of anger and aggression in my house back in Connecticut. The origin of that anger stems from my dad's past history and the existence of my half siblings. My motivation for going to college comes from seeing my parents struggle my whole life, even until this day. I flew out here, checked out the institution, and I liked the atmosphere. The city seemed pretty laid back and so I decided to transfer out here and now I'm just continuing my career. (Interview, April 2, 2013)

Educational Aspirations

I believe that education is important because it's a stepping stone to everything. Starting from language and ending with professions, including trades, and I mean education is basically passing knowledge from one to another, so it's an essential part of everyone's future. I don't feel unaccomplished in my life, but it feels like it takes so long to get what you want. Especially when you enrolled in college, it seems unreachable. I should be a junior now, and I'm like a sophomore/junior. I know that currently I am doing a lot of people than those who drop out of school. To obtain your education and pursue a degree is being resilient. I got into a lot of trouble in high school. After I finish my degree, I would like to go back and find all the kids that are and were just like me. I barely graduated high school with my class. I never got into any sort of crazy trouble, but I was always suspended; I failed twice and I still graduated on time. School

at the time was tough. I basically had to do two years in one. I want to show kids

that you can do it, even though it's hard, it's still possible. (Interview, April 2,

2013)

The Graduates

Five

>   *Determination, dedication and motivation.*
>   Five

Background

My name is Five. I grew up in Irvington, New Jersey. I am a 26-year-old Black

man. My education started in Irvington. In high school, education was never a

priority; it was encouraged by my mother. I grew up in a single parent home,

with three other siblings, so the individual attention to each child wasn't present.

My mother did the best that she could with the circumstances that our family was

given to make sure that each child felt loved. I speak so frequently about my

mother because she is a great part of my educational journey, because of the

struggles and the hard work she endured. She always made sure that we had food

to eat and shelter, even if it meant sleeping in an abandoned car or on the back of

someone's porch. Due to all of these things, our family went through, my mother

is my motivation. In high school I wasn't really focused on school. My grades

were a representation of my struggle at the time. My academic struggles were due to multiple factors that affected kids in my community. I was raised in an environment of gangs and drugs, overcrowded populations, and not enough resources to help poor families.

I played sports as well which developed another motivation to succeed. Prior to my junior and senior year, I was a product of my environment and became active in a gang. My grades did not really start to come together until junior or senior year. I realized during that time that there were two roads which I could travel. First, I encountered a near death experience during a drive by shooting, where I could have been killed. Surviving that experience I realized that this was God's way of showing me that he was giving me another chance at life, to start over. Once I eventually overcame the stupidity of my actions, I chose the second option. I used my mother's struggle as motivation and the fact that my younger siblings were looking up to me as a role model. My goal was to get into college, and I was focused on making education my priority.

I started to attend day school as well as night school predominantly to get my G.P.A up to qualify for college. I attended public high school during the day and I enrolled in a Muslim-sponsored night school for two years. Prior to going to night school, you could say I was an average student. I maintained a 2.0 to 2.1 G.P.A, the American College Testing (ACT's) was not offered to students in low-income areas, so all we had to take were the Scholastic Aptitude Test

(SAT's). With the assistance of night school, I qualified for Division 1A colleges and universities. I became nationally known for my football and track abilities. Top Division 1A schools like Indiana and Rutgers University began to take an interest in my abilities until they caught wind of my grades prior to night school. The top university, which I signed a commitment to play football for out of high school, dropped me because of my grades. In 2005, I decided to attend this institution because my coach in high school had connections to some of the college team's football coaches. When I arrived, I had to first attend the community college for a semester and then I was placed on a full ride athletic scholarship. From 2005–2010, I received the All Academic Honors Award, for three years straight. I also received the All Conference and the National Academic Honors Reward in 2008.I have also received numerous awards for my community service and academic honors as well. (Interview, March 21, 2013)

Educational Aspirations

The reason I decided to attend college was to prove to myself and others that I was willing, capable, and determined to succeed. I did not want to become a statistic like other people from back home who chose different paths, like the one I could have chosen. I knew I wanted to become a better person, and to do what no one else in my family had ever done, attend and complete college. I wanted to be a better role model to my family, my siblings, and everyone else who looked

131

up to me. I want to give hope to those who come from the same walks of life and influence them to not go down a path that involves deception and mistreatment of other people. Finally, I really wanted to prove to my mother that she raised a man and her hard work paid off. Today, I have a bachelor's and a master's degree and I serve as a liaison and advisor for many different on and off campus organizations. I just recently created another non-profit organization dedicated to helping the community and encouraging other young men and women to get involved. My education is important to me personally because I come from an area where education isn't highly regarded. For a man of my type, African American, without education there are many limitations. Even with education there are still limitations, but there is a farther role that you can take being an educated Black man or a woman. (Interview, April 2, 2013)

Percy

> *It always seems impossible until it is done.*
> Nelson Mandela

Background

My name is Percy. I identify as a 26-yearold Black female. My educational journey began in Trenton, New Jersey where I was born and raised until the age of 10.I went to a Catholic school from grades 1–5. I tested out of kindergarten and was therefore always the youngest person in school among the rest of my classmates. Even at the age of 10, I was always expected and was expected by my parents to continue my formal high school education, even after high school. I moved to the southwest shortly after 5th grade. I attended three different middle schools in two different cities located in the southwest. One I attended very briefly and the other I resided in to finish my middle school education. I left the first middle school promptly due to bullying and continued my secondary education because the expectation remained that I would always finish school no matter the circumstances. In high school I begin to form a better idea of what I wanted to do with my life. Art had always been very important to me; however, I begin to find the areas of video games and movie development to be the most appealing. I took college courses during my high school years in my field of interest. My high school had a vocational program partnership with the local community college.

I desperately wanted out of this current city after high school. The option of enrolling in the local university meant that I would have to stay here. Residing in this current city seemed like such a commitment at the time, and four years seemed like forever to a seventeen year old, high school senior. Therefore, I decided to enroll in a technical school in a one-year accelerated program. I attended a film school in Canada for two years. The first year I was in a foundation art program and the second year in a classical animation program. A majority of my classmates seemed to get jobs after graduating from this program in the area of reels. I, on the other hand, returned to the United States. I returned to the community college located in the southwest and shortly after enrolled within the four-year degree program on the main campus of the university in late 2007. I bounced around the college of arts and sciences for three years searching for my place here at the institution. I then changed to another college on campus, and to this day, I still feel out of place. I feel that as a person of color and also a creative person, I have never found my place here at this particular university. There is probably an art program somewhere out there for me that I would enjoy and would probably enjoy having me as a student. I never felt that any major I have been in at this institution even remotely wanted me in their department or wanted to see me succeed.

There has been a strong lack of advising at every college. I also feel as though I have been consistently shoved off from one person to another. I always ran into advisors who would say to me "I don't know, go talk to someone else". I always encounter a negative attitude when I am dealing with administration and professors who have accused me of plagiarism. I did not finish in four years, because this campus did not help to provide a very linear or straightforward situation. I hated being back in this city and back at this institution.

In less than a month, I will complete my degree program with a long overdue bachelor's degree in individualized studies and a minor in studio art. I still have no idea what the hell a bachelors of individualized studies means at this institution. My greatest worry is what does this kind of degree sound like to an employer. An employer doesn't know me from Adam; all they see me as is a resume, and to them I am a stranger during the interview. My emphasis is fine art printmaking, which I would like to expand on further in another study, like a concentration in a graduate program. However, I feel a great trepidation about spending more money on higher education after my experiences here at this institution. My love for learning is not strong enough to justify more possible agony. I feel education is important because it is something that can never be taken away from you. You know, they can take your life, your clothes but what you have retained as knowledge, that can never be taken away, that can never be stripped from you. (Interview, March 21, 2013)

Educational Aspirations

My education is a median to provide opportunity for more people that are like me. I want to be there to hold the doors open for someone else. Since I've walked through it, I'm going to hold it open for someone else. I definitely believe that it's, a well worth it thing to do. When you've succeeded, you can't just be like well, you know deuce bitches and leave those who are just as disadvantaged as you to fend for themselves. That type of mind frame just does not work. There could be another awkward kid, artistic kid like myself who enters this environment and feels completely discouraged, and if they don't find

a support system or find the strength within themselves, I want to help them

fight, to find something to hold them here at the State College of the Southwest.

You know, I don't want them to end up flipping burgers or fucking around in the

street? I certainly don't want to go back to living in my old neighborhood in

Trenton. I have faced enough adversity. I know that I have to give back; there is

no other option. (Interview, April 2, 2013)

TEN

> *History is a people's memory, and without a memory,*
> *man is demoted to the lower animals.*
> Malcolm X

Background

My name is TEN. I was born and raised in Compton, California. I am a 36-year-

old Black man. My earliest memory of education that I can recollect begins in

the first grade. The year was 1982 and I would walk to school from 48th to 58th

and Western in South Central, Los Angeles. At the time I was attending Western

Street Elementary. I never remember walking to school with my mother, who

had given birth to me at the age of 15 and never finished high school. Between

1980 and 1982, President Reagan's war on communism and Nicaragua, better

known as the Iran-Contra Scandal exploded in South Central. I'm a historian, so

throughout this story, I will integrate my history into my educational journey.

Now, back to my story, during this time in history, the streets of South Central were flooded with massive amounts of cheap cocaine and a new way to cook the drug. Many people refer to it as crack rock.

Reagan's industrialization and deregulation left the poor and insignificantly educated in Los Angeles vulnerable to the new drug industry. My mother soon became a victim of the new capitalist market. She was ill-equipped and not informed about the downside of this drug. When I awoke in the morning, most of the time, my mother was unconscious or absent from the house. I would get myself ready for school. As a result of her condition, I walked those 10 blocks to school alone. I did not mind being alone on my walk to school due to the fact that my mother was a crackhead. I remember being teased by neighborhood kids about my mother being a crackhead, but I had no idea what that term meant at 6 years old. I remember my mother at the time was physically so small that she would wear my jacket. One day, on my way to school, I was walking through the alley. I remember it was very cold outside so I put my hands in my jacket pockets. I found what I knew helped turn my mother into a zombie at night, a crack pipe. I remember thinking if I smashed the pipe, my mother would be ok and everything would change. I smashed the pipe and scattered the pieces on the way to school.

There were some times when my mother would come up to the school. I remember our school having a Halloween parade. I was walking in a circle around the school in my homemade karate kid outfit. My mother had done the best she could to make the costume and even took the time to make the headband. She was there at the event, and I also remember her being the loudest parent in attendance. All I remember her screaming was, "That's my baby". At 6 years old, that was very embarrassing. I remember thinking that school was my refuge. I saw the school house as my escape; it was my path to a new life. School was never about what I learned; it was always about the new life.

Two years later I moved to Compton, California. I completed elementary, middle school and high school in Compton. The walk to school was cathartic, but the walk home was dangerous, especially when I entered middle school and high school. In middle school, I found sports. I was a smart kid, but without the support from the school, and trying to do homework at home was a challenge. Compton at the time was the gang capital of the world. I was approached to join a gang in middle school, but at the time, I was viciously opposed to gangs. All of the programs like Drug Abuse Resistance Education (DARE) really worked for me while I was in school. Such programs, as well as seeing my mother go through so many things, had really driven me to the point where I did not want to deal with the street life.

I discovered track and field; this was the one thing I could do after school at the time. In high school, I would walk to school with my football coach. I'm including all of this information to explain that school was not just about learning. My educational journey did not emphasize the importance of the books I was reading or the stuff I was learning. School was never about the bullshit; it was about walking away from the life I was living to become something better. School was always a place that was special to me, because I would watch TV shows like the Cosby Show or A Different World. In these shows, people always attended school or college; by watching them, I knew that if I did something in school, I would have a better life. The only problem I had was that I wasn't too good at academics because I didn't like to do my homework. I'm a historian now in a PhD program. The one thing that has kept me going is one simple question: Why is it that my mother was in the condition she was in as well as many other people within our community? With time, I have figured out the answer to this question and now I want to go beyond. The question of why do these things happen to our communities kept me going throughout my college career. Whether I was in elementary, high school, or college it never mattered – I was trying to run away. I decided to come to the southwestern region because I wanted to get away from California – I was running away. I knew that California was a trap for me at that time.

I joined the Reserve Officers' Training Corps (ROTC) program. After I received my master's degree, I enlisted in the army as an officer. Now I'm getting my doctoral degree. My educational journey has always been about trying to fix what was broken in my life. The journey has also been about knowing that I am better than all of the shit that I, as well as my friends, have endured. Some of my friends dropped out of high school; some of them simply chose to get a job after high school. I applaud their efforts, but at the same time, I knew that this was not the route I was supposed to follow. I believe that I am supposed to save the world. Therefore, education is important because it's the singular way to upset the cart, to fix what's broken. (Interview, March 21, 2013)

Educational Aspirations

Poverty is just a stepping stone. I want to use my education to fight for the kids who come from the same circumstances I did when I graduated from my high school. I was ranked 5th in the nation when I entered community college. I was third, when it comes to running back and kickoff return. I had the physical talent but I wasn't prepared academically. I'm fighting for those kids who have the ability but do not have the training to deal with the rest of the obstacles in life. I've proven that you can do it throughout my life. I had up to 50 kids from Compton coming to the State College of the Southwest. This university rejected them and ostracized them and did not embrace the diversity they brought to this place. Also, I am always fighting for myself. I embrace that kid that follows behind me, that wants to change his life, who wants to be something better, who wants to change the trajectory of poverty, in his or her life. I want to inform them that you can do it by simply going to college. I mean college is the easiest thing you could ever do compared to trying to find something to eat or a place to call home. There are so many hard things to do; college is one of the easiest. The problem is if you're not prepared for this new environment or whether or not it's prepared for you. College life could also eat you up and turn you into something that you are not. This environment can make you look like something you're not. I'm one person; if I can get two kids to graduate out of those 50 that I have, that's an accomplishment. I have about three kids who are within a semester or two of graduating out of that first class of Black kids from Compton. So if I can find 10 at a time and have a program that develops them I guarantee you I can change where I come from. Just by bringing those kids here and having them go back and dedicate their efforts to helping the community. Even if they don't go back to Compton, they still will not be there causing trouble. Education is important. So if you were born into poverty, education can be the one way that you can change the trajectory of a family, of a generation. (Interview, April 2, 2013)

Chapter V

Crystallizing Thematic Stories

Reflections of critical assertions through the testimonies of the study participants provided substantial opportunity for the evaluation and affirmation of the campus climate in State College of the Southwest. The story constructed by the institution is one that embraces diversity as an essential precondition for achieving excellence (State College of the Southwest, 2013). The university's portrayal is consistent with the forefronting of capitalizing on the voice of every student, by showcasing pictures of so-called multicultural collaborations throughout the campus. The contingency of claims of equality and equity are based on foundations of student-centered learning and student success. The data presented in this chapter addressed the research questions of the study presented in Chapter 1 and Chapter 3. These testimonies interpret various experiences that occurred in various social, administrative, and academic environments. The experiences of these participants are constructed to counter the constructed majoritarian narrative regarding diversity as stated by the institution.

In this chapter, I will rely on counter story as a method to present the racist and exclusionary experiences of Black students with regard to the academic and social practices at the forefront of the institution. A fictional character called Busara[12] (Swahili

---

[12] Busara is my fictional alter ego. He symbolizes an oft unrecognized striving of my double consciousness, my two-ness, one that embraces a lens that enables a different internal reality (Du Bois, 1903). He is epitomized as a narrative to reinforce the historical and present quests of Black students for

translation for wisdom) has been employed to represent an alternative narrative in the tradition of Black feminist and critical race scholarship and other literary works. Busara is a symbolic representation of my subconscious. He will be summoned sporadically throughout the chapter to only engage in dialogue at junctures to remedy confusion or facilitate reiteration and reaffirmation. The scene of the counter story was realized during the research process and has been narrated through the first person omniscient perspective. The construction of the counter story was a result of crystallizing the data into thematic units. The crystallization process was invaluable in the construction of this counter story. The data of multiple perspectives in relation to the same scenarios and participant interactions with matching entities crystallized the formation of the themes (Lincoln & Denzin, 2013; Richardson, 2000).

The chapter comprises multiple speaking parts, including the participants' dialogue with each other and the researcher, and an omniscient voice of the researcher's, quilted by the researcher's field notes and journal entries. The qualitative research

---

racial justice in educational institutions. He was inspired by Derrick Bell's (1987) alter ego Geneva Crenshaw who surfaced in *And We Are Not Saved: The Elusive Quest for Racial Justice* and Richard Delgado's (1995) alter ego Rodrigo Crenshaw from *The Rodrigo Chronicles: Conversations about Race and America*. Busara, who no longer acknowledges his birth surname, was born as Busara Smith in Detroit, Michigan and grew up on Mack Avenue and Helen Street. He graduated high school from Blanche Kelso Bruce Academy-Depaul. He attended college at Morehouse University in Atlanta where he graduated Cum Laude and received a B.A. in African American Studies and a minor in Economics. He then continued to graduate school at the Barcelona Graduate School of Economics and received his Masters in Economics of Public Policy, subsequently returning to the doctoral program at Harvard University to receive his Ph.D. in African American Studies – he graduated first in class. Throughout this chapter, Busara is engaged in dialogue about topics related to my research practice. Busara assisted in the deconstructing of institutional and structural discrimination, historical and modern day manifestations of systematic racism.

methodology allowed the researcher to study the participants in their classroom and natural settings, while attempting to make sense of the phenomena of the study (Becker, 1986). Field notes were incorporated in the narrative to bring the participants' stories to life through the counter story.

The Introduction

I was working intensely through the historical document analysis phase of the research study, sitting in my cubicle in the College of Education. During the retrieval of my documentation, I started browsing the university website. I decided to search the word "diversity". I came across an interesting document – an assessment completed in (2008) on the historical and present vision of the university and its current ranking in multiple facets among other national universities. As I read through the lengthy report, I noticed the institution's use of the word "diversity" in various areas of the report (Field Notes, March 27, 2013). As I sat in silence contemplating why I had researched this word, Busara made his appearance. Busara's tall, dark, six-feet, ten-inch frame towered over my chair and glared at the computer screen. His dreads dangling over the top of my head, I could hear him sucking his straight pearly white teeth. I immediately looked up to acknowledge his presence as he read the search engine results on my computer, courtesy of the school website. Busara stated:

> Is this institution actually representing diversity strictly on race? The pictures
> overshadow the position of racism as a decomposition of cultural integrity

144

illegitimately displayed through this type of media portrayal. Ladson-Billings (2001) refers to diversity as the recognizing and understanding of the cultural and individual privileges of those who are different from the dominant group. The differences in diversity refer to categories of race, class, gender, educational background etc. (Banks, 2004).

Busara glanced down at the report I was reading and then sat on the counter next to mine so he was facing me, looking at me as if waiting for me to respond to his initial question. I decided to respond and tread gently as I knew this could turn into an all-day affair, one I did not currently have time to become fully invested in. I responded:

Throughout the report, the university continuously reverts and solidifies to a "long standing commitment to diversity in all forms". I agree with your statement regarding the illegitimate portrayal of diversity. I believe that the ideological presence of diversity is one that overshadows oppression and creates unawareness and leads to a non-articulation of discrimination (Brock, 2005; Kincheloe & Steinberg, 1997). We both know that without data, statements are merely that, statements. Research is needed to confirm facts and for real accounts of such experiences to hold water. Currently, I am conducting research to investigate whether or not these actual accounts exist in our institutions or are merely imaginary. I will keep you posted on my data collection and analysis.

Busara flashed me a hearty smile. He gave me a thumbs up, curling one of his dreads with maroon ends, and then disappeared into thin air. I continued analyzing my data. I was preparing for my interview session scheduled for the following day.

As I was waiting for the last participant of the first group to arrive, I glanced around the room at Percy and TEN and then at my watch for the second time. Five finally arrived at the door, greeting everyone and walking to the chair at the far left side of the table. He sat down, leaning back in a comfortable position, awaiting further instruction. Percy, who had been engrossed in her journal, looked up from. TEN, working on the seventeen-inch computer screen of his laptop, noticed the silence in the room – he also looked up and began to stare in my direction. Their collective intensity was palpable and so was their eagerness to share their stories – in response to the questions I sent to them five days prior to the interview session. I glanced at my journal and reviewed the objectives of today's interview. I explained to them that they would share their stories with regard to their academic and social experience as undergraduates at the university. The data collection procedures in my study required I distribute the interview questions a week prior to the study. The questions I previously sent to the participants asked them to write about their experiences in the following areas: a) campus activities, b) student housing, and c) campus advising. Considering the long-standing commitment to diversity constantly embraced by the university, I began the interview process (Field Notes, Interview 1, 2013).

146

Racial Microaggressions

In this chapter, I will incorporate the theoretical frameworks of critical race theory and Black feminism to deconstruct issues of racial microaggressions the participants in the study encountered in the State College of the Southwest. Microaggressions signify subtle insults (verbal, nonverbal, and/or visual) directed toward people of color, often automatically or unconsciously (Solórzano et al., 2000). Marable (1992) defined racism as "a system of ignorance, exploitation, and power used to oppress African-Americans, Latinos, Asians, Pacific Americans, American Indians and other people on the basis of ethnicity, culture, manner-isms, and color"(p. 5).

Trends of Apathy and Alienation

In a school of let's say 25,000, I know it's more than that but let's estimate the population is 25,000, because I don't know the exact number. We are only going to get about 250 out of that 25,000, that 10% is including professors, staff, and everybody else to participate in anything that we try to get done. I think because I'm not of the predominate race here it causes a conflict of interest to others. I have a crowd of diverse people, Black, White, Hispanic, but the majority people are still isolated in their own norms. It is rewarding when we get people to understand and embrace diversity to help everyone to come to an understanding. Whereas you have a whole lot of others on this campus who aren't willing to take that same steps. (Five, Second Interview, April 2, 2013)

147

Five volunteered to go first. He sat up in his chair, placed his hands on the table, crossed his fingers, and waited for me to confirm that he had the floor. I looked at the other two participants. Before I could engage the other two participants to see if they had any objections, Five had taken a deep breath and began speaking. I grabbed my pencil, started to write in the notebook in front of me, and glanced at the digital voice recorder to ensure it was functioning correctly (Field Notes, Interview 1, March 21, 2013). I was at this time fully committed to capturing the story of every participant. Five started, appearing earnest:

> I have a lot to say about this situation. I can testify about a negative experience
> that I had with the student government here on campus. We did a proposal for
> funding, so that we could receive money to put on events for Black history
> month. We took our proposal to the diversity board of the student government
> here at the university. Basically, they (the diversity board) ate it up. They asked
> questions like: why are you all bringing this person here, who is this for, who
> will be in the crowd? What about the rest of the university. The performers we
> were bringing in were to help this campus celebrate Black history month, so we
> were embracing our roots and the performers that we brought in were for that
> purpose. Basically, they tried to disregard our whole proposal because it wasn't
> the normal Hispanic groups, or White cowboy groups that normally are brought
> into this university. We told them that our events were projected towards

everybody, not just Black people. We tried to bring in everything that would show diversity, we did open mic night, a comedian, multiple artists, and even had an art show. It seemed like even though we said this, they were only for White groups or Hispanic groups that usually come. There was a very negative presence of aggression that was coming towards our group. The questions that we had to answer, you know, the way that they (student government representatives) were talking to our group, I was on edge. I felt disrespected. It's supposed to be open doors and for us trying to bring our culture and open it up to this university, I felt like it was a slap in the face. We sit here all the time and are open to the stuff they bring to campus. Why does it involve such harassment when we try to bring something different or more diverse? (Five, Graduate, Interview 1, March 21, 2013)

At this time Percy, who is also a member of the student organization that submitted the proposal, changed her body position as if she wanted to speak. Percy was paying full attention to Five's testimony. At this time, I was not aware that she had been part of the same event. Percy unfolded her arms, nodding in agreement with Five. After Five finished, she looked away and stared at a blank spot on the wall behind me. She then shifted her glance to the wall, deep in thought, and focused her attention on me. When she saw the moment of silence, she immediately interjected (Field Notes, Interview 1, March 21, 2013):

Well it's interesting, I happened to be there in that meeting as well as Five, who already described to a tee what had happened. I also did not feel respected. I saw some eye rolling, what seemed to be some irritation when we were proposing our program for the month. You know I am the one who kind of likes to watch the watcher. So as things were being presented, I wanted to see. It was interesting to see the kind of reactions that we were getting. I was excited about our programs. So I was shocked, I did not expect to get those types of questions we were getting that had a very condescending tone. They said things that I felt were downright openly rude. I felt that this was because they do not consider us [Black students] to be on the same level that they are as human beings. I did not feel that I was on the same level of welcoming or respecting or held at the same level of respect as the other diversity groups that were in the room. I felt that this was because they do not consider us (Black students) to be on their same level. I did not feel that I was on the same level of welcoming or respect as the other non-Black diversity groups that were in the room. (Percy, Graduate, Interview 1, March 21, 2013)

Journal Reflection (Date: 3/21/2013)

Five and Percy explained how they felt as if they were placed beneath the other students, who they described as all non-Black, on the student government diversity panel. I recognized the ideological presence of discrimination that provides an

150

awareness of assumptions that attempts to make Black students feel as if they are second-class students. Kendall (2006) talked about perception in embracing a White privileged normalcy when defining the characteristics of a college student. Kendall referred to the "normal" college student's visibility as a mirror reflection grounded in White privilege. I could not help but reflect on Kendall's work while such experiences were being shared as testimonies. Their testimonies relayed a sense of inferiority and the mental impact of the microaggressions they encountered through the actions of the student government.

Davis (1989) defined racial microaggressions as "stunning automatic acts of disregard that stem from unconscious attitudes of white superiority and constitute a verification of Black inferiority" (Solórzano, 2000). The belief of superiority and White privilege is often a subtle presence legitimized through the dominant groups' ideological values. The right to dominance and inherent superiority these participants described in this meeting can be found in Audre Lorde's (1992) definition of racism. Five described the moment as "the way that the student government talked to our group was from the experience of someone who was not used to going outside of the cultural norm here at the institution" (Interview 1, March 21, 2013). The fact that the Black student organization faced aggressive and disrespectful racial comments before a non-Black diversity board operationalizes Manning Marable's (1992) definition of racism. Marable described racism as a notion beyond the binary discourse of Black and White to include

151

multiple races, their experiences, and voices. These definitions, in collaboration with the participants' experiences, forced me to embrace an alternative lens into the subtleness of institutional racism.

While I sat in the black leather reclining chair, I could not help but notice the white walls that surrounded the room. The saying "if these walls could talk" immediately struck me – what would they say regarding the stories they heard here today on the university's commitment to diversity. Little did I know at that moment that this was not only happening to this small group of participants. I would learn more that day about previous encounters with the same student government. During the interview session with my second group of students, I heard similar stories from two of my participants, Danie and Unknown.

The sun had begun to set, it was getting late. But I was still fully consumed by the research process. I was now in a session with my second group, the ones who had at one time or another separated from the university. Danie and Unknown were also former officers of the Black student organization two years prior to Five and Percy. They referred to incidents with the student government body from their time. The experiences they shared were from a time when the department was in the process of rebuilding its student organizations on campus. Unknown leaned back in his chair and looked down at the brown shagged carpet in the room. He was deep in thought for about for five seconds. He then adjusted his satchel on his right shoulder to sit comfortably in his

152

chair. Once he was comfortable, he was ready to share his experience (Field Notes, Interview 1, March 21, 2013). He explained:

> Something that will always stick out to me is when I was a part of Black Programs and we were trying to get Black Programs back on the market. Black Programs at the time had been very inactive due to the lack of student leadership. Administrators, who worked in campus activities and student government, were making it so hard for our organization. There were times when they would give us the wrong deadlines and then we'd miss the due date and miss out on opportunities. There were also times when we thought that we had paperwork complete, and the student government would give us something else. Like a task we had to do to make sure our proposal would get accepted. They were really giving us a hard time and I didn't understand why. (Unknown, Pushout, Interview 1, March 21, 2013)

Danie looked at Unknown and nodded in agreement. She stared at her journal for a moment and then raised her head (Field Notes, Interview 1, March 21, 2013). She noted:

> I remember being denied funding the first time we submitted [a] proposal. I remember the same experience but it also came down to paying our performers. I remember, this one performer came to our school and he did not get paid for a very long time. We had already finished the proposal, which was a challenge in

153

itself to get approved. The process for the approval was intense and even disrespectful towards our group (Black Student Association) in particular. His agent was constantly calling our department. The process to pay this man for his performance did not go through the system until almost eight weeks later. The legal adviser for our department ended up going over to the student government office and fixing the problem, because they wouldn't listen to any of us. I felt as if the student government and the staff in that office did not care. It was as if they (the student government) did not want to see a huge turnout for Black Programs. (Danie, Pushout, Interview 1, March 21, 2013)

After hearing the participants' stories and later reviewing the transcriptions, I ran into my office and pulled out multiple literary works from the shelves. Overtime, I had collected various scholarly articles related to some of the issues I was hearing in my interview. To gain a better understanding of the outcomes I was learning with regard to the participants' testimonies, I knew that I needed to obtain and fully comprehend previous research and data concerning this phenomenon. I grabbed literary works of critical race theory, Black feminism, and other articles collected together strategically, thanks to Staples, and began to review literature. I noticed multiple highlights, notes, and tabs placed in sections of different articles, and I started my review of the literature in those sections (Journal Reflection, March 21, 2013).

Before I could even fully collect my thoughts, I heard heavy panting behind me. I turned to find Busara drenched in sweat, hunched over with his hands on his knees, trying to catch his breath. I laughed at the sight of him in all white clothing. His panting and the dirt covering his shoes were piquing my curiosity. I asked him, "Are you ok old friend?" He spoke:

Who you calling old? I'm 39 years young. I've been out running with the bulls in Pamplona, Spain. In the middle of my run, I sensed that you needed me and just as the bull was catching up to me, I got out of there and teleported directly to you. So explain to me what seems to be troubling you.

I related to him everything about Danie and Unknown's experiences and how they preceded Percy and Five's by two years. I told him how I was amazed when I analyzed their testimonies, as all four participants shared similar experiences. He shook his head and enlightened me about some interesting facts. He stated:

What's happening to these participants is shared in multiple literary works. Rovai et al. (2005) refers to the experience related in the testimonies of Percy, Five, Unknown and Danie. Rovai explained there are both cultural and interpersonal trends that negatively affect the academic performance of Black students. The learning and execution of prejudice is extremely influential on the educational outcomes of students of color (Allen, 1985; Bennett, 2002; "Persisting Racial Gap", 2004). Bennett (2002) explained that the learning of

155

prejudice can be exemplified in the behavior of staff, students, and faculty on college campuses. Behaviors that categorize and practice "othering" of students of color create a cohesive cultural force which can negatively influence learning and define societal behaviors. Black students report a higher rate of significant racial-ethnic conflict with multiple campus entities on predominantly White campuses (Ancis et al., 2000).

Busara patted me on the back, crossed his arms, and smiled. He said, "Dear Cheryl, you will figure it out, go back to the literature, let it be your guide". He then once again vanished into thin air before I could ask him another question. I returned to the articles. Midway through the first 20 articles, I came across the work of critical race theorist Daniel Solórzano. According to Solórzano (1998), the components of racism exist at both micro and macro levels. As I read the article, I was reminded of an experience shared by TEN, one of the participants.

TEN quietly listened to the stories shared by Five and Percy. At the beginning of the interview, he stated that he would like to share his story after the other two. While listening, he constantly looked to the sky and circled his hands over his face. He repeatedly adjusted the collar of his polo shirt, shaking his head. Every so often he glanced at his laptop, which he later informed me contained notes from his journal; he would intently scan the screen. Throughout the interview, I noticed adamant expressions of frustration and slight anger; he shook his head in disappointment, sometimes nodding

156

in agreement with the other participants. When there was a brief silence, he looked at Five and asked if he was finished. When Five gave him the nod, TEN shared his experience (Field Notes, Interview 1, March 21, 2013).

I want to go to the macro level and look at that incident that happened here when I was an undergraduate. This predominantly White fraternity decided they wanted to display the confederate flag at the stadium during the football game. I mean I felt as if this campus thought it wasn't on the administration or student government to actually do anything immediately at the time of the incident. I see it as they, administration and the fraternity, felt that it was OK. The department of Black Programs decided to hold a press conference. Even at the meeting afterwards it seemed as if administration felt that there wasn't anything that needed to be done. It was as if they were saying "OK let's talk about this a little and then nothing else more needs to be done". So I think the atmosphere is such that things like that are OK. That kind of atmosphere bleeds into everything else. For it to be at a homecoming game, that's pretty bold. I felt a lot of anger. When you're such a small population in academia and you deal with things like this head on, you feel helpless and hopeless. Your first reaction is anger; the kind of anger that you feel when you're in the streets, where you need to defend yourself. Due to the atmosphere that is here at this institution, it is what exists. It's OK, we're going to cover up a little bit, but that's it. There are not going to be any suspensions or anything like that, it was a harmless gesture I guess.

(TEN, Graduate, Interview 1, March 21, 2013)

After listening to TEN's experience, I proceeded straight into my second group session. Four days passed after the first session of interviews or any sighting of Busara. I had been listening to recordings of the interview sessions repeatedly on my laptop. I was reviewing the transcriptions when something unique caught my attention. I immediately walked over to my wall of post-it notes to review possible themes. I felt a cool breeze of air on the back of my neck, and without turning around, I acknowledged Busara in the room. I said, "Hello my good friend, back from Spain already I see".

Wordlessly, Busara walked up behind me, reached over my shoulder and placed his hand on a pink post-it note. I followed his hand and the post it was under one of the themes that had emerged during my data analysis. It was highlighted with a participant's name in the study, Danie. It stated the page number and section of information transcribed during the first interview of group 2, the push-outs. I noticed a highlight from transcription number two and had to go to my field notes to try and recall the moment that involved a testimony from Danie. I looked at my notes and reviewed what had occurred at the time of the interview.

Danie was sitting in her chair with a look of anger on her face after Unknown finished telling the group about his experience. She had just checked her cell phone. I

158

was wondering if she was looking at the time or texting another party. Once Unknown stated that his testimony had ended, Danie stated angrily:

> I feel sometimes the university tries to hide a lot from the students when it comes to race and racism here at the institution. Administration just does not deal with the issues. They don't try and bring the school together, they don't try to bring awareness of racism here and I don't think that's fair. We are in a different time, in a new generation; we're paying attention to things that are going on here on campus. We need to be enlightened instead of the State College of the Southwest hiding these issues that are affecting us, because it's not fair. (Danie, Pushout, First Interview, March 21, 2013)

When TEN referred to the lack of representation of Black people in academia, I began to think about studies performed by Hale-Benson (1986) and McWhorter (2000). Hale-Benson and McWhorter's research discussed the absence of a strong Black presence on college campuses and how the issue strongly impacts the achievement gap between Black and White students in higher education. When I spoke to TEN, he informed me that the administrators at the institution overlooked the incident and only a panel had taken place, called by the department of Black Programs. Danie and TEN had the same sentiments about the university's lack of effort towards racial micro and microaggressions. It is interesting to note that Danie enrolled in the institution during the 2010–2011 fiscal year and TEN in the 1998–1999 fiscal year. TEN graduated from the

159

institution several years prior to Danie. During my review of the transcriptions, journals, and notes, I noticed in multiple group sessions testimonies regarding the low Black student representation in the institution. In these testimonies, a trend of experiences surfaced in which the participants recognized a diminution of their identity and an undermining of their epistemological value. Steele (1992) asserted that the devaluation of Black students in education has directly affected their educational experience (Brock, 2005). Participants throughout this study discussed similar experiences.

Epistemological Racism

The disconnection of identity from historical accomplishments can stunt the scholarly growth of human beings; this constitutes epistemological racism (Asante, 1991; Matsuda, 1988; Schuerich & Young, 1997). As time passed and we were nearing the end, Five was finishing his testimony on the second to last question of the day. The testimony about his past was so potent that a small moment of silence took over the entire room. Everyone had shared touching stories and experiences, and at that point, I was ready to ask one of the last questions. I inquired about their biggest challenges on campus as Black students. TEN sat back in his chair, placed his hands in front of his face. The room stood silent. I told the participants that I would give them a minute to reflect on this question. After about 90 seconds, TEN inhaled deeply. Without looking in my direction, he stated (Field Notes, April 2, 2013):

I think the biggest challenge is finding out who we are as Black students and what it means to be of African descent in a world that isn't predominately that, especially in America. And I put it that way because, you know, being Black on a campus doesn't really mean anything. Understanding that you have a sort of root, or a foundation to yourself and that your roots are what are most hated. Understanding that on a campus where you do not have a singular class that specifically deals with African descendants in the United States. There is not a Black history class here on this campus, but they have a Master's program. I mean really, what does that say about the program? I did some research on the history program or the history department here and there's not one person I'm not going to say of color, a person of African descent in the history department. I mean they have enough money to have a Master's program but they will not give up funding to support a Black history or African history course, let alone major. The excuse that it is because of the need is definitely not viable because you have two professors that deal with China. The Asian population is less than the Black student population. You have three professors that deal with Europe and then you have two people that deal with the history of the southwest and so on. The challenge for many Black students on this campus will be finding out who they are, because that's what college should be about, whether its self-identity or professionally. Becoming universal, that's what the word university means. So the hardest part is going to be about finding who are and what that means is you're going to have to search yourself, not yourself individually but you're going to have to find out yourself, what that means and that's going to be difficult because there not a lot of tools here. (TEN, Graduate, Interview 2, April 2, 2013)

Percy placed her hand on TEN's shoulder as he made his last statement. She had been making contributor noises and giving signals of support such as thumbs up or a head nod during his testimony. When TEN wrapped up his last statement, she asked Five if she could go next. He gave her the go ahead and she started to speak (Field Notes, April 2, 2013).

I'm also going to kind of steal a page out of TEN's book. College is about finding yourself. Your 20's are a fun decade of a stew of shit that you learn. You know you're trying this hat on, you're trying that hat on, to see which one actually fits. I mean we start doing that a little bit as teenagers but largely the process happens when you are becoming a young adult. And when you enter post-secondary institutions, you still have no idea who you are as a person. So for an African American, someone who identifies as African American, on a university campus, especially a place like this with such a small Black population, there's not much to reach out to. Thank goodness that we do have Black programs in a support capacity, but let's say you want to reach out to your heritage and find out more about your identity. Well you know this school would have you think that you don't have one, you don't have an ancestry. We can learn about Tom, Dick, and Harry, you know everybody from zonga history to almost everywhere else, but here Black people don't have one. The university makes it seem that the message to us is that: your kind is not important enough for us to even talk about in the curriculum. The only mention I have of Black history is a small blip in recent American history with regard to slavery and then small blip talking about the Harlem Renaissance during the 20's–30'sand the civil rights movement. These historical moments are told from a perspective of Kumbayyah where we are singing and chanting and marching together. I mean other than that, there is not a real discussion of the African diaspora in America. It's just not really important and the university makes us feel like we are invisible and just kind of here. It's like the university says to us you are here but you don't matter. This kind of message says a lot; without saying anything. (Percy, Graduate, Interview 2, April 2, 2013)

Percy and TEN in their testimonies offered their perspective on epistemological racism. As the notion of epistemological racism resonated in my head, I knew I needed a break. I decided to go to the bathroom and wash my face and hands. As I was doing that, I looked up and stared in the mirror – Busara was sitting behind me on the toilet tank, his legs crossed, leaning against the wall. I said to him in a snarly tone, "What do you want?" He smiled and said, "You're overwhelmed, talk to me about what's on your mind sugar plum". Feeling the need to vent, I immediately started without hesitation:

So during the analysis phase of my research, the notion of epistemological racism emerged. Patricia Hill-Collins (1991) stated that there are four characteristics to understanding Black men and women and they are as follows:

- Concrete experience as a criterion of meaning

- The use of dialogue in assessing knowledge claims

- The ethic of caring

- The ethic of personal accountability.

Black feminist Patricia Hill-Collins (2000) also explored the White elitist discourse of knowledge overshadowing the identity of Black people by promoting mainstream privileged ideologies that render Black history inferior and almost invisible. Busara nodded and stated:

So what you're telling me is that this phenomenon you are investigating is allowing the emergence of past accounts of historical racism continuing even now and accepted academically in our institutions? The question you have to ask in your research is: How can you utilize the soulful words or language of experiences continuously inferiorized in academia because of the race of the speaker, and make it meaningful? This question applies to you, because it is your inherited responsibility. You are standing on the shoulders of those souls who preceded you, they form your foundation. From critical race theorists like Derrick Bell, Gloria Ladson-Billings, and William Tate to Black feminists such as Audre Lorde, Patricia Hill-Collins, bell hooks, and Angela Davis. Let us not forget Carter G. Woodson, Booker T. Washington, and Cornell West[13]. These scholars, along with many other scholars of color, have created spaces for you to answer this question. As it resonates in your mind, you have to know that Black epistemologies are legitimate, but the question should not only be whether or not they are legitimate and meaningful to you, but to whom?

I opened my mouth to demand a clarification but before I could utter a sound, he vanished. Once again, good ole Busara had stated his claim and left me hanging alone with my thoughts. As I referred to the literature during the reviewing of my transcription, I recalled stories I had heard during the second interview session with students currently enrolled in the institution. At this time, I was in the process of creating a wall of points full of post-it notes. My wall contained notes I had taken from the literature I was reading, highlights from each transcription, and field notes from the interviews and observations. The incorporation of this wall made the process of crystallization easier. After Busara's reality check, I found myself constantly rearranging notes and post-its, and by the second set of interviews, I had memorized

---

[13] Busara mentioned these scholars to remind me that there are plenty of Black scholars who address racism and other forms of subordination in various capacities and I must follow in their footsteps.

many of the highlights. I opened up my transcription from this session, checked my wall for notes I had previously made, and analyzed my field notes. I knew that I needed to dig deeper.

Diminution of Self Identity

Having just walked into my house from a day of work, I flipped on the light right next to my door. I jumped as I realized Busara was sitting on my love seat with his legs crossed and long arms stretched. He greeted me in his deep baritone voice, "Hello young Ingram, how are you doing?" I contemplated whether or not to answer this question because I could not decide on its sincerity. I answered strategically, "I am fine, Busara, how are you doing? I see you look refreshed, where have you been?" I knew he was awaiting my question. He had a knack for reading my thoughts. He answered enthusiastically,

> I decided to take a trip to the DuSable Museum of African American History in Chicago. I have always wanted to visit and witness the exhibits dedicated to great leaders throughout our history. I recommend every person to experience this place to acknowledge some of the great strides Black people have made throughout history. I was intrigued by their dedication to the very diverse struggles, accomplishments and to acknowledge so highly the accomplishments of Blacks throughout history. There was one exhibit called "Reflections", dedicated to renowned individuals whose lives and careers have addressed the

166

fundamental political, economic, and social realities of the 20th century and beyond (DuSable Museum of African American History, 2013). This exhibit got me thinking about identity and the presence of invisibility. I think about how African Americans or as you prefer, Black people, have been stripped of their identity and reduced to a colonized history told from a dominant White perspective (Berry, 1994; Hooks, 1981; Woodson, 1930). It amazes me how much we don't know about our own history that could redefine our identity.

When Busara mentioned identity, it instantly took me back to my recent encounter with the meaning of identity during an interview session with my participants. I told Busara:

Bauman (1996) addressed identity and how the concept has continually been reconstructed and redefined. Bauman stated that modern society enables the disappearance of identity, leading to a loss of control if one tries to radically shift their identity. In a post-modern society, the issue with identity is avoiding the fixation of one particular identity and keeping the option open. Racism, dehumanization, and cultural deformation of a people can result in false feelings of helplessness and inferiority (Boske, 2010; Collins, 1986, 1998; Crenshaw, 1989; Matsuda, 1993). Jennifer Russell (1993) also described her self-diminution as a Black woman in the legal academy of a predominantly White institution. During my interview sessions with all three groups, I inquired them about their

167

biggest challenges on campus as Black students. A major theme that emerged during the crystallization process fit into the category of self-identification and feelings of disempowerment that the participants experienced in relation to race and placement.

Busara was sitting attentive on the couch now, his legs no longer relaxed. He said in calm, intense voice, "Tell me about these themes". I decided to share with him some of my experiences by recalling the scene of my previous interview.

Cherise was seated at the far end of the table to my left, deep in reflection about her experiences in class on campus. She removed her iPhone from the top of her journal, tilted her head, and began to flip through the pages. She mumbled as she read her notes, trying to find the right moment when she could begin expressing her contribution. She flipped her hair to the side as it was falling over her shoulder and blocking her view. I realized she had found her starting place when after almost 20 seconds of silence, she began (Field Notes, April 2, 2013).

> I don't know what the percentage is according to race and enrollment at the institution, or how many Black students are here, but I look around and I'm the only Black student in the class. For me this is a challenge, because it makes me feel like I'm alone. Even though my professors try not to create any indifference in our class, it still matters. (Cherise, Currently Enrolled, Interview 2, April 2, 2013)

About 37 minutes passed as I listened intently to the experiences of three students currently enrolled in the institution. Gilbert, on my right, steadily rocked backed and forth in his chair. I originally started the dialogue with Cherise, because Gilbert had requested that I come back to him about his curricular experiences. He felt he was not ready to immediately answer the question and asked me to pass. After Cherise, I glanced in his direction. He smiled at me and said he was ready to share his story. He placed his hands on the back of his head and leaned back in thought. With his head pointed upward, he said (Field Notes, April 2, 2013):

I once took a chemistry class here at the university. I would sit in class and look up and notice that I'm the only Black guy in the class. This makes it hard to speak up sometimes. I don't know why, but even if you have a simple, question or something, you just don't really feel comfortable. During class, a majority of the time I would just hang back. If I really don't know what's going on, I would ask the teacher in private or email him. Whereas other students seem to participate more, but yeah, like she said, you kind of feel alone. You always feel like your voice is powerless. (Gilbert, Currently Enrolled, Interview 2, April 2, 2013)

At this moment, Cherise sat up in her chair, folding her hands on the table. She and Gilbert began to engage in dialogue as if I was not present there. They had established a common ground about their curricular experiences within the institution.

169

The powerlessness statement made by Gilbert had triggered a thought in Cherise. At this moment, I could feel a sense of engagement and vulnerability they were more willing to share because they were not alone in their experiences (Field Notes, April 2, 2013). Cherise stated:

> I feel like the institution has done a great job of making Whites and Hispanics
> from this area feel so comfortable. We constantly see events where others are
> wearing their cowboy boots around campus. The university does not put forth
> any real effort to make Black students feel comfortable; they make us feel like an
> outsider. Even when you try to go to the event you are made to feel by other
> organizations that it's not for everyone, only certain people. The university
> employees, student government, the staff, all put together their own activities. I
> don't like that. I feel like the Black students who do attend this university are
> bold because of so many obstacles we have against us by the institution.
> (Cherise, Currently Enrolled, Interview 2, April 2, 2013)

Gilbert was nodding in agreement, making direct eye contact with Cherise. He placed his hands on the table and pressed his fingers down as he leaned forward. He stated:

> Especially the concerts and they have different activities all the time. Many
> Black students are left wondering what hell, like we don't exist. I'm from the
> East Coast, like the colleges back there, they get many diverse groups to

perform. Even the small colleges have diverse activities, they host all sorts of big name hip hop artists. I'm pretty sure a lot of White students listen to hip hop and would attend a concert if we had one on campus. I'm sure such events would bring a diverse group out to support, but the opportunities are never presented. Eighty to ninety percent of the events I hear about is something that I would never even think about getting off my ass to attend. (Gilbert, Currently Enrolled, Interview 2, April 2, 2013)

Cherise and Gilbert's concerns have been defined by Robin Barnes (1990) as a complex delineation of social interaction that Racially Stigmatized Identities develop as a result of differing cultural viewpoints. The feelings of exclusion are formations that create a climate of racial hegemony. Racially Stigmatized Identities are continuously reminded by institutionalized racism that their existence and concerns in comparison to Whiteness are of minimal value and constitute that of the "other". The testimonies of Cherise and Gilbert also address the problem that marginalized groups maintain a familiarity with the silencing of their voices, especially in classroom spaces (Lorde, 2007; Valencia & Solórzano, 1997).When speaking with students who had been pushed out of the institution about the same topic, Polo and Danie shared similar thoughts and experiences.

Stereotype Threat

Stereotype threat is defined as a social psychological predicament that can arise from widely known negative stereotypes about one's group. The existence of such a stereotype means anything one does or any of one's features that conform to the stereotype, making it more plausible as self-characterization in the eyes of others and perhaps even in one's own eyes. We call this predicament stereotype threat (Steele &Aronson, 1995, p. 797).

Aronson and Steele (1995) address the notion of stereotype threat as a process of examining the situation threat that derives from a broad dissemination of negative stereotypes. The presence of stereotype threat undermines the academic achievement of Black students in post-secondary educational institutions (Aronson & Steele, 1997; Aronson & Inzlicht, 2004; Solòrzano et al., 2001). During two different group sessions, participants related encountering situations related to this definition. The following counter story will testify to the participants' experiences with stereotype threat on the campus of the State College of the Southwest.

Danie, Unknown, and Polo sat at the table in silence. Unknown had just left the room briefly to go to the men's bathroom. As we sat at the table, I decided to break the silence. I asked participants to explain what it's like to live in their skin while attending the institution. Polo was the first who was willing to respond to my inquiry. He touched his hand as if he was acknowledging the color of his skin. I wondered if his actions were part of his reflection as he seemed intrigued by the question. He stared at his skin with a look of concern but expressed his seriousness as he started to respond. He then placed his mini laptop on the table, leaned back in his chair, and peered at the sky (Field Notes, April 2, 2013). He stated:

I feel that this institution has shown me that college is a battle of differences, ethics, and morals. To be in my skin is a very different experience on this campus. On this campus, there are a lot of students who will never understand what living in my skin really means. Being in my skin I think I'm challenged every day. I'm one of the only Black people in all of my classes, the only Black person in the majority of my classes. I feel as if my teachers love me, and they love to hear my perspective. When it comes to other students, I feel as if other students are offended by my responses. You get the feeling that when you speak up in class that some students are intimidated because of the color of my skin. You get the feeling that they believe African Americans to be ignorant or that we do not have a lot of education. A majority of the time we don't feel accepted. And that just leads you to being alone because we (Black students) don't even come together as a collective group. So if you don't have an African American group or programs to back you up, you feel alone, which affects your education. (Polo, Pushout, Interview 2, April 2, 2013)

Journal Reflection (Date 4/2/2013)

Polo's statement was an example of internalizing an immediate situational threat unconsciously initiated from the negative stereotypes he encountered about Black students (Steele & Aronson, 1995). This is an example of a racial campus climate where manifestations of marginalization and discrimination contribute to the academic oppression of Black students (Hale-Benson, 1986; Kincheloe, 2004).

Danie sat and watched Polo the entire time he relayed his story. I could not help but notice a look of concern that crossed her face. Prior to Polo's statement, I felt she was disengaged, buried in her cell phone. She started to change her position from leaning back in her chair to sitting straight and attentively. She clasped her hands together loudly and her gaze had then shifted from Polo to me (Field Notes, Interview 2, April 2, 2013). She noted:

> I agree with him and what he had to say. It just feels the university has African Americans here for sports or like stats, but they don't want to give our student programs real resources or help. It sometimes feels as if those that are here trying to get an education are really discriminated against as opposed to those who are playing sports. I feel like the university really does not want Black students here. They only want us to exist for their benefit. The university does not want to do the things that benefit our population. Administration does not want us to learn

anything; they just want us to remain uneducated. Ever since I have attended this school, this is how I constantly feel. (Danie, Pushout, Interview 2, April 2, 2013)

Unknown started his testimony directly after Danie finished sharing her experiences. He stated:

I was with a friend and you know how friends sometimes are just crazy, or having fun with one another. We were just two guys hanging together waiting for class to start and we were playing games with one another. There were no violent actions or even physical violence of any sort occurring or anything. We weren't putting our hands on each other. My friend walked outside of the door and I closed the blinds on the door. I was standing in the hallway. I just closed the blinds so I wouldn't see him flicking me off or whatever cause that's what he was doing. Then there was this lady, I believe she was a secretary in the office of the building. I think she was someone that sits at the front desk. She was Caucasian as well. She told me that I could not touch or close the blinds. I told her that I was sorry, and then I did not touch them after that, I complied. Then about 10 or 15 minutes later a security guard walked up my friend and I. He was Hispanic. At this time, we had been sitting on a bench waiting for class; we probably had about 5 to 10 minutes until the class started. He asked my friend and me if everything was good. We told him, yeah, and assured him that we were just playing and that everything was cool. After that, I didn't think anything of the incident. He then stated that "someone in the office was complaining that you guys are having an altercation, and that you guys are being very disruptive." I told him that he had the wrong people, because we were not causing any disturbance. He's told us that he had a witness that stated that we were causing a problem. He had literally walked into the building and came right up to us without talking to anyone else. I asked if we could speak to the witness to see if there was a problem or to clarify what he was saying at the time. He then really starting making things up, by stating that my friend and I were involved in a physical altercation and that we were fighting. I told him that we were not fighting and that I was waiting for my class to start. I walked into my class and the security guard decided that he wanted to follow me. He was continuously asking what had happened and I continued to inform him nothing of that matter had happened. He's then asked if he could have my name. I then informed him that he could not have any of my information because I had no idea [of the] fight he was referring to at the time. He continued to stay in my class and harass me in front of all the other students. He then stood in my classroom and called the police on me. I then decided I should leave class, so I walked out. I never talked to the police. I left because I knew that if the police arrived, they wouldn't have listened to my side of the story. (Unknown, Pushout, Interview 2, March 21, 2013).

Danie's testimonial immediately made me reflect on the notion of interest convergence in critical race theory. Derrick Bell (1992) stated that interest convergence is a term that identifies with the advancement of Black people in the United States and how it always coincides with the self-interest of elite White people. Danie, Unknown, and Polo's testimonies corresponded with the value and capital the institution places in Black students. By the end of the interview, I was feeling overwhelmed and ecstatic about the information I received during the session. I was realizing that these participants were sharing experiences that placed them in a position where they became agents of change to their socially conditioned constructions of knowledge (McLaren, 2000; Wertsch, 1998). After an hour, we wrapped up the session. It was getting late and I needed to get some rest. I packed up my black leather single strap bag and headed to my car, hooked the digital recorder up to my stereo, and turned the radio on auxiliary mode. I placed my book bag in the back seat. As I turned on my headlights, I saw Busara standing in front of my car, his hands on his hips. I opened the car door and motioned for him to get in my vehicle. He complied and jumped in; we listened to the interviews all the way home. I knew I was in for a long night of reading, discussing, and analyzing data.

Exclusionary Practices in Campus Housing

The following day, I entered my office and sat down in front of my computer. I had invited Busara to work with me but he declined, saying he had a hiking expedition in the Swiss Alps. The night before Busara and I spent hours distinguishing the social and academic experiences of the participants and arguing about their meaning. I had developed a game plan for my day of research at work. I started by researching the perception of both the academic and social values of the university through multiple forms of data collection. I began my plan by viewing every college within the institution's website, including strategic plans and visions. I also analyzed the university's presidential institution-wide strategic plan and vision for the next four years. After analyzing multiple reports, I decided to venture into the social settings of the university. I came across the following information on the university's housing website: "Studies show time and time again those students who live on campus are making a choice that positively impacts their lives, enriches their day-to-day interactions, and makes their educational experience more fulfilling" (State College of the Southwest, 2013). I was intrigued. I opened my locked cabinet of data and pulled out the transcriptions from earlier interviews. I remembered that many of the participants had actually taken into account their experiences with housing on campus. I decided it was important to share testimonies not in line with this statement. I went back to an experience I had during one of the interview sessions.

TEN was running about five minutes late. He had sent me a text message stating that he was riding his bike to the interview and was running behind. I informed him that I would wait for his arrival before I started the interview session. Percy and Five were discussing an incident in which Five was reported to the director of Black Programs for harassing the student government about paying performers. As I was just about to join them, TEN came running through the door, sweaty and out of breath. He apologized, then took an open seat at the table. I asked him if he would like a cup of water and he said yes. After allowing time for him to catch his breath, he started to settle down. I started with my first question regarding their experiences with on-campus housing (Field Notes, Interview 2, April 2, 2013). I asked the participants to tell me about a positive or negative social experience within campus housing. TEN started first:

I once mentored a program that brought in over 50 Black children from Compton. The students were having an issue with the administration in housing. I was called into a meeting by the administrators of the admissions and housing department. Instead of the meeting going in the direction of what can we do for these students, or with the students from urban areas, it was more of a lecture to me kind of taming the wild beast in these kids. It led to a lot of other problems with the students because the housing administration began to label this group of young Black children as the urban kids. Even if they weren't from urban areas but were friends with kids who weren't from that area, they all begin to be courted off and partitioned from everyone else. They were placed in the position of the "other". What then happened was the kids saw this, they were very perceptive. It caused a lot of problems but those problems wouldn't have happened if the administration had an attitude directed towards helping the students. Instead they looked at them as the "other" and played out that scenario. Residential Assistants (RA's) began to isolate these students. Then you have whoever is in charge of the RA's beginning to coalesce; they began to create this idea; this identity for these "urban" kids. While this is happening, these kids are doing what everyone else in the dorms is doing, but because these kids are doing it, now it's a problem. (TEN, Graduate, Interview 1, March 21, 2013)

TEN's statement about conforming students to negative stereotypes by the housing administration, undermining their potential, was troublesome for me. Steele and Aronson (1995) refer to the conformity of these students as a self-fulfilling possibility, a result of a negative racial campus climate. I was in a dilemma, because it seems the trajectory of blame is more dominant among campus housing administration. At the same time, I had to evaluate my subjectivity within this situation (Journal Reflection, March 25, 2013).

Five and Percy were both writing in their journals as TEN was speaking. Five glanced around the room, leaned back in his chair and put his pen down. He waited briefly to ensure that TEN had finished his testimony. He peeked in Percy's direction, who was still writing in her journal (Field Notes, April 2, 2013). He stated:

A prime example is I speak to everybody. I'm a social person. I speak to Caucasian, Hispanic it doesn't matter. Let's say for instance I speak to you and it's a hello and that's it, no further communication. I witnessed a Hispanic or Caucasian person speak to an RA that they didn't know and the conversation would go on for five minutes. They find anything talk about, I mean you can hear them providing different resources to them that would help them on campus, that they didn't even ask about. That information they provide for that group, I could use to, but I never get that opportunity to experience it directly. I've seen it a couple of times since I've been here at this institution. (Five, Graduate, Interview 2, April 2, 2013)

Stanton-Salazar (1997) stated that institutional agents such as teachers, professors, and peers can provide resources that increase the opportunities crucial to the college experience of students of color. Five referred in his testimony to how resources provided to other non-Black students could have been helpful to his education as well, but he was never approached with the same opportunities by the housing administration. Five expressed his sentiments about the discriminatory actions of the housing staff and dealing with information that creates a lack of opportunistic resources for students such as him. Percy and Renee also shared similar stories from a different perspective about the same entity.

Percy was fully attentive. Her had put her pen on her journal and was staring right at Five. She had finished writing and reflecting over her notes and was ready to share her perspective. As Percy placed her elbows on the table and intertwined her

181

fingers, Five wrapped up his testimony. I stared in her direction and gave her a nod (Field Notes, April 2, 2013). She stated:

> I almost lived on campus; there was a time when I got as close as even picking up a key to move into my room on campus. There was a problem. I went to go pick up the key to the room. When I stepped inside of the room, there were a lot of broken things, the room was not clean. I did not feel like it was ready for me to occupy. So I relayed that back to housing. I told them, you know what, this is unacceptable. I want to dissolve this contract unless you have some other place that you can put me. This is not at all what we agreed on, I did not sign up for these standards. This room is below my standards and should be below yours as well. When I was going to relay that message there was this White girl in front of me. It was at the beginning of the semester, when people are checking into their rooms and there are lines everywhere with people who have problems. I don't know why but this assistant director of housing who was having this conversation out in the open with the girl in front of me. It was the same type of situation. It was more like the girl you put me with was not to my liking and she just couldn't share stuff with her. She stated how she just could not handle living with her anymore or sharing a living space with her. She had also just picked up her key and was in the process of moving in but she just couldn't deal with her roommate. Apparently she wanted to acquire another living space. The assistant

director was very sympathetic and she said quietly, but apparently not quite enough because I heard it, "we are going to pretend that you didn't pick up your key," because normally they keep the two hundred dollar deposit. You can still get out of your contract but they still keep the money. She says oh it's ok I understand. She (the assistant housing director) was very personable, very sympathetic, and so she made that deal with her. I went to speak to her, and she was like no, not going to happen; you already picked up your key, there is nothing that we can do. I was just like wow. I believe she was Caucasian or a very light-skinned Hispanic. She seemed like the very nice girl and apparently I did not come off the same way. I didn't appear to the housing director to be the all American girl next door who by golly just made a mistake and they just didn't want to put in any sort of distress. However when I came up to the counter I expressed that my freezer door is broken, this place is nasty, you obviously didn't clean up after the last person. There were things on the sheet, which I went over with the girl who took me to the place, and they were completely disregarded. I said you know what, the situation is very unprofessional. It was almost as if she was shocked that I felt this way. She still had the same attitude of this is the way it is and this is what was going to happen. I had to have my dad come up to campus and speak with the administration. I ended up moving back to my parent's house and commuting to school because of this experience.

(Percy, Graduate, Interview 2, April 2, 2013)

After a week of waiting for transcriptions for all three sessions of my second interview, I started reviewing the data. I was listening to experiences with on-campus housing, and I noticed an extreme similarity between Percy and Renee's stories. I started to retrieve the data with Renee's group and found a pattern in the behavior of campus housing administration. Renee had been sitting very quietly during the interview session. She was always very engaged in her journal while other participants shared their experiences. Shortly following Cherise's story, Renee blew her nose and held her finger up to get my attention. She was ready to share her experience as well" (Field Notes, Interview 2, April 2, 2013). She stated:

My freshman year my first roommate was Jane Doe (pseudonym); she was like over 6'2" nearly three hundred pounds and was eating all my food in my dorm, to the point where I had to lock up my food. When I first got there, she didn't have any friends, and I made a group of friends. She didn't like my friends; she just wanted to hang out with me. She told me that she did not want my friends in the room, so I blew it off, I was just like my friends are allowed in the room; it's not just your room. So she went to campus housing and campus housing calls my phone and explains that I can't have my friends in the room and I was like well where is this in the rules? So I blew it off, I ended up going to the front desk and

184

asking the housing administration if they could just move me into another room. They refused, like we went there several times, and they refused, and finally Jane Doe moved out. So they moved this new girl in my room, this White girl, she had a boyfriend and she was never in the dorm room. Then, maybe a month later, I get a call from campus housing saying that, they got an email from her saying that she felt threatened by me. That her life was threatened and that she needed to move out, but she was never here. I never even had a personal conversation with this girl. The assistant housing director informed me that if the campus housing administration had to move another roommate in my dorm, they would remove me from the dorms. Period. I just called my dad, who lives in another state, and he got mad and then he called the housing director and the rest of campus administration. After the administration had talked with my dad, the assistant housing director was all apologetic. I didn't understand, like when I had asked to be moved out of my room, they wouldn't allow me to move out but when they (the previous roommates) asked, they were moved right away. I was mad; I was so frustrated when it first happen I cried. I was like I don't understand why they let her move out when I had to go up there several times. I went to everybody and they wouldn't let me move out of my room, but when the White girl goes, it's a whole different story and then I'm threatened to get kicked out of the dorms. (Renee, Currently Enrolled, Interview 2, April 2, 2013)

I was fascinated by the similarities between the two participants' testimonies. Percy and Renee's were three years apart, 2007 and 2010 respectively. Polo and Unknown also shared similar experiences from the fiscal year 2009–2010 with housing administration during their interview sessions (Observation Notes, April 8, 2013).

It was the second interview session and the dialogue between Polo and Unknown ventured into their experiences with on-campus housing. Polo had actually volunteered to share his experiences first. As he sat up in his chair, he took off his glasses and placed them on his journal in front of him. Polo started to speak about an experience from the 2009 academic year:

> A negative experience I've had was with the housing administration when I lived in an on-campus dormitory. It was regarding the directors and some of the staff there and most of them were on the student government committee. My first couple of days here I moved into the dorm, and some of my things came up missing. The only people that had access to my room were my suitemate and my roommate. I filed a complaint and the housing administration said they would investigate the situation. A week later there was still no report or anything that came back. I went to the head of campus housing and made another complaint and nothing still happened. I had to change my room. The housing department made me pay extra money to change rooms, and then they stated that they never received anything on file about me, making a complaint when I had made two

different complaints. Then I realized that when I finally paid for my new room, my suitemate had a similar situation. Due to the fact that his parents were involved, administration didn't make him pay to get his own room. They moved him immediately, and it just seemed like everything that happen for him was done properly. When it came to me filing a complaint, it was always an issue, something was always going on, either the paperwork wasn't there or they didn't want to file my complaint. When I did the paperwork or made a complaint, they just said make another one, but then weeks later, the problem would continue on and nothing would happen. (Polo, Pushout, Interview 2, April 2, 2013)

Unknown was listening intently during the interview to Polo's testimony. He was always very laid back, but he stared at Polo during his story and never once broke eye contact. I can recall that the majority of the time when people spoke, he kept his head down and would only raise his head to speak when it was his turn. In this instance, his body language was somewhat different. When Polo had finished his testimony, Unknown, who never actually looked at me during his story, began to speak about his experience with housing (Observation Notes, April 8, 2013). He stated:

Something that sticks out to me happened when I first came out here for school as a freshman in the southwest. I had heard about the school through a friend. I ended up talking to an advisor and he reassured me that I had a place to stay when arrived on campus. That was not the case when I got out here, and

187

basically I was homeless. I had my bags and nowhere to go you know. While I'm out trying to get something to eat on campus or get around the university to talk to someone, my bags were sitting wherever I could find a place for them. I was enrolled in school, and I didn't have anywhere to stay. Later that evening, around six or seven at night, I finally get a room one of the dormitories here on campus. The problem with this situation was that I was living in temporary housing, so I ended up having to live with like five other boys, for almost three weeks to a month. Then campus administration finally threw me into another dormitory. The housing administration also charged me for moving into another dorm on top of the charge for temporary housing. I ended up moving the dormitory they threw me into after living in temporary housing because where they put me at was just so loud and hectic, I just could not sleep. So, I ended up moving out of that dorm two weeks later. I was charged another fee. (Unknown, Interview 2, April 2, 2013)

All of the testimonies in this thematic unit occurred under the leadership of the same housing director who has been at the State College of the Southwest for over six years (State College of the Southwest, 2013). As my inquiry continued on the housing administration as part of my document analysis phase, Busara decided he wanted to join me. As he slid up next to me, he rested his lanky but trim figure on the arm of my desk chair. I knew by his body language he was itching to speak. I looked up at him as he spoke,

> As students of color transition to living quarters on campus, social acceptance is a key dynamic in their educational success (Astin, 1993; Tinto, 1993; Hurtado & Carter, 1997). Harper and Hurtado (2007) demonstrated in their research that the unwelcoming and non-acceptance of diversity can result in the isolation of underrepresented groups throughout a college campus (Hurtado & Carter, 1997). Theories of college departure by Tinto (1993) and involvement by Astin (1993) explained that adjustment to college for diverse students entail adjusting to unfamiliar social as well as cultural contexts.

I immediately agreed with his intellectual contribution to my current investigation. I responded:

> Campus housing represents a foundation of support for students during the transitioning process. The campus housing ideology is one of acceptance, no matter student classification and/or status; this is a place that embraces "every" student (State College of the Southwest, 2013). As stated in the testimonies of Polo, Renee, TEN, Percy, and Five, there are counter stories to this housing ideology of diversity and acceptance. This type of data is a prime example of the fictitious commitment to multiple facets of diversity, especially in the practice of acceptance and embracement. Diversity itself has become a dominant

189

westernized ideology in need of deconstruction (Brock, 2005). The image of diversity is positively built on socialized constructions that overshadow negative contradictory actions by campus leadership.

Busara stood up and clapped enthusiastically. He patted me on the shoulder and flashed me a slightly mischievous grin. He said, "You have come a long way, young lady". He then reached across my laptop and typed in the word expectations in Google scholar. He smiled at me and stated, "Onward we march, souls in heads and armed with knowledge". I smiled back and nodded.

Academic Perspectives and Expectations

The vision being reinforced by the university is that the advisor will assist students in planning their educational degree program. Advisors' duties involve connecting students to external and internal resources that promote educational success while attending the institution (State College of the Southwest, 2013). While students are responsible for maintaining their academic programs, the university posits that it is the advisor and staff's job to assist them in making good academic and career choices. The counter story following this introduction will address the university's publicizing of the advisor's responsibilities to students.

The Role of Advise in Degree Completion

I could hear the howling of strong winds and the rustling of leaves through the office walls. The interview room had no windows, but the conditions outside spelled the approach of a dust storm in the southwest region. All three participants had reached on time, and we were now gathered around the table in the middle of the interview session. I had just posed the participants a question about the academic experiences of students in relation to their advisors on campus. I was prepared to hear their testimonies. I had my notebook open, and I was writing vigorously, taking in their stories. I was thankful for the Olympus digital voice recorder, because of its ability to catch all the information being shared by the participants.

I glanced at the recorder and noticed that the participants had been in session for almost 33 minutes and 47 seconds. I just posed my academic advise question to the participants. TEN was the first to volunteer. He politely asked Five and Percy if he could share his experience first. They both gave him the go ahead and he started:

When it comes to advising, again I deal with all kinds of students; you will see

that being an advisor, you can set them up for failure. The way that you do that is

that you load them up with all kinds of classes. I have seen this happen on more

than one occasion. Now if it was done maliciously, I don't know, because it's

kind of hard to engage what's in an advisor's heart. You begin to see this happen

over and over again and you notice that there's a pattern. I have worked in

advising and in admissions as an advisor, and being a part of the recruitment

team, there are certain areas that the departments will decide to cover and other's

that they won't. You know, you only have so much in recruitment dollars, so that becomes an excuse for advisors to not cover a certain area. For example when I was a part of a recruitment team I would go to the north side of Compton and go to the actual school. The way advisors get around that is that they say, well I went to this specific college fair and that covers me for not having to go to particular a place like Bouie or Andres. Places where you know you are going to get a lot of students who need more academic and financial help than others. They may be first generation Americans, let alone first generation college students. What I saw happening was areas where the students were considered wealthier, economically speaking, had a personal contact in advising. When I stepped outside of that pattern and started establishing relationships with students that were not "worthy" or "wealthy", I got a response from my superiors and colleagues of well, you spend a lot of time with those kids, why don't you spend more time with the kids who basically deserve your time. (TEN, Graduate, First Interview, March 21, 2013)

While reviewing TEN's testimony over and over, I felt frustrated. I could not believe what I was hearing. I was outraged by this story and felt instant anger. I yelled out in a fit of rage: *Busara where in the world are you when I need you?* Busara's face instantly appeared on my computer screen. He looked alarmed at my outburst, his eyes bulging, his eyebrows raised. He held his hands up in front of his chest and asserted:

192

Simmer, Simmer, Miss Ingram. I know that this journey is not easy – it takes time, patience, study, and even meditation. TEN's story relates to research performed by Walter Allen in 1987 that states that the recruitment and retention of Black students remains at the bottom of the priority list of a majority of colleges and universities in the United States. Black students have been labeled unworthy of recruitment and are less likely to receive recruitment from post-secondary admissions (Allen et al., 1991; Pruitt & Isaac, 1985; Solórzano et al., 2000). Pruitt and Isaac displayed the recruitment process of narrowing channels according to institutional systematic discrimination on the basis of race and privilege. This is not only happening at your institution, but across multiple institutions (Pruitt & Isaac, 1985; Solórzano et al., 2000); it doesn't start or stop there. You must maintain a sense of urgency and also dedication toward your cause but remain level-headed. Your fight is not of singular action, it is a struggle faced by many in the past and today. You have just begun to take your place as a scholar in the making in this long-term struggle. The thing you have to remember is that when you do stand in that place, you remain firm, fixed, and unmovable.

I looked into his dark brown eyes and felt a sense of calmness spread through my body. I covered my face in frustration and stared at the screen in complete silence. I stood up and walked over to my post-it note board. I looked at the orange post-it that contained literature to support the emerging themes, and something caught my attention. I read the information and let it sink in. I then turned to my computer screen where Busara was still watching me, and I spoke:

> The privileges of recruitment discrimination towards students of color are mirrored in objective standards such as minimum test score requirements and subjective screening criteria (McDonough & Antonio, 1996; Swail et al., 2003). After hearing and rereading TEN's statement in the transcription, I decided to go to the admissions advising and recruiting website for prospective students. I carefully viewed the staff profiles and pictures listed on the site. There were a total of 10staff members listed as admissions advisers. A total of 80% of the advisors were from the actual southwest, and the other 20 spent a majority of their professional life in the city where the institution is located. I noticed that all 10 advisors graduated from the institution in the study. There was no profile listed for a Black advisor within the department. Only 40% of the profiles listed where they did their actual recruiting and out of that, all of the advisors were assigned to the southwest region. The decision to include this type of observation stemmed from Pruitt and Isaac's (1985) research, who referred to the "old boy network" in college recruitment practices. The practice of the "old boy network" refers to TEN's statement concerning exclusion while recruiting of students from low-income educational institutions located in heavily populated Black

194

neighborhoods in Compton (Bowl, 2001; Thomas, 1981). I cannot believe this shit! I am fed up with the foolishness that is taking place. I know what you mean when you say taking my place in this research movement. I have to continue to arm myself with data. I will go back to my transcriptions and continue to read more.

Busara replied with a smile, "You are starting to think like a researcher my dear friend, peace out". And he was once again gone in a flash. My computer screen turned blank. I resumed my work immediately and started analyzing.

Immediately after TEN finished his story, Percy did not hesitate to share her experience with the advising office. She did not even wait for a cue:

I started out with one advisor who I guess quit, so I was inherited by another advisor who was ten times more negligent than the first one. This one I almost had words with. I always had to chase her down, always calling her, emailing her, going to her office. I felt like this woman was literally the fugitive. She tells me that she is always incredibly busy and that there are two other advisors even though her name is on all my information. I received an email telling me this is who you go to now. When she was trying to push me off on all these other advisors I should have known, a light should have gone off telling me that this woman is going to be a problem. I had to get to know another advisor, and I told her I wanted do to 19 credits in both the spring and the fall and she told me "why do you want to graduate like that". The advisor told me why don't you just wait and petition to graduate in the fall or in the summer of the following semester, why are you trying to push it. I told her I've been in school for a damn long time and it's time to get out. I'm running out of financial aid and I have loans I need to pay back. I mean if they didn't run this place like a business, if administration wants to treat this place as a business and not a school, you're selling the product, I'm a customer. This is what I want, I want to be able to do my thing and just get out of school. The advisor and I went through this again this semester. (TEN, Graduate, First Interview, March 21, 2013)

I was in the process of reviewing the transcript of the last group of the day when something caught my attention. I was reading through page fifteen when I noticed that Renee had spoken about the same issue TEN referred to in his previous testimony: "advisors who were setting students up for failure". I found it interesting that the two participants were in different groups, separated by almost 16 years of enrollment, but were describing the same issue from different perspectives (Field Notes, March 23, 2013). Renee, who was in a different group from Percy also had a troubling experience with her advisor.

Renee sat up in her chair about 40 minutes into the interview session. She was staring directly at me as Cherise was finishing her testimony. She noticed that Cherise had completed her story and began (Field Notes, April 2, 2013):

196

I had a major problem with my first advisor, freshman year. I was chemistry

major with a minor in forensics, and I was told at orientation that I shouldn't take

math and English within the same semester because I was already taking

chemistry. I was told at the orientation that it would be an overload, so then I

went to go see my advisor. He wasn't listening to me; I was trying to tell him

what the admissions department had told me during orientation. I didn't want to

be overloaded my freshman year cause they said a lot of people dropout their

freshman year, especially Black students. I had English 111, Math 190, which is

pre-calculus trig, Chemistry 115, and Government. I went into the advising

office, to see the same adviser, because I was stressing myself out. The course

load was weighing down on me, so I was asking him is there any way that I can

drop a class. He (the advisor) informed me that I could drop a class but I couldn't

pick up another one, because it was the middle of the semester. I have enough

credits to withdrawal, but I can't pick up another class. I was like isn't there

shorter classes, isn't there eight week classes? He did not give me any feedback,

he was looking at me like I was stupid so I just got up and left. I failed every

class that semester and lost my financial aid. I had to work extremely hard to get

it back and I was thankful for my parents because they paid for my education

during this time. (Renee, Currently Enrolled, Interview1, March 21, 2013)

Renee explained that if it had not been for her parents' financial support, she would not have been able to finish school. Renee's statement that parental involvement both socially and financially is strong influences the attainment and completion process for students in higher education (Cameron & Heckman, 2001; Perna & Titus, 2005). Contradictory to the works of Cameron and Heckman and Perna and Titus, two out of three graduates in this study came from extreme conditions of poverty and two out of three students who are currently enrolled also came from what would be considered financially poor families. Statistics reveal that Black students are more likely to take out student loans and receive larger Pell grant awards as opposed to White students (NCES, 2011; Perna & Titus, 2005). To receive student loans and Pell grants, students were required to maintain a 2.0 G.P.A. I had to consider the question: what would have happened to Renee if her parents did not have the money to support her education? The issue in Renee's case was that because her grade point average had dropped, she was ineligible for any financial aid assistance. She stated, "I do not know where I would be if I had relied on my advisor, he set me up for failure. Being a freshman I didn't know any better".

Cherise was listening to Renee's story. At certain points of her story, Cherise would look up and then return to writing in her journal, as if Renee's story was bringing back her own experiences. Cherise was shaking her head while writing. Once Renee had finished her story, I turned my chair in Cherise's direction. She looked up at me and started to speak (Field Notes, April 2, 2013):

When I first arrived on campus, I came in as a regular student but I had college credits back home. I was registered for a class that I later found out that I had already taken. I was later going to get the credits transferred over because I had received a passing grade. I was looking to get those college credits transferred over here so the university could accept the credits. I was enrolled in an eight-week course the second half of the semester. So, I went to my advisor and I asked him, will I have to pay financial aid back, basically, and he could not give me an answer, and he gave me his business card. I gave him my number. He never called me, and I was afraid of that cause I thought you know, maybe I would owe financial aid money because at the end of the day, I had to withdraw or drop that class and then I was under the full-time student requirements. So I was scared that I would have to pay the university back for that class. I took his business card and after emailing and calling him, leaving voice mails, I never heard from him. This whole scenario was like the second or third situation from this same guy who I'm going to for assistance that can't help me. So I was pretty upset about everything that had taken place. (Cherise, Currently Enrolled, Interview 1, March 21, 2013)

Chandler (2008) and Swail (2003) stated that a nurturing environment for Black students, including guidance and other means of academic support, can positively influence the Black student achievement rate. Percy, Renee, and Cherise all shared stories that reflected the absence of advisors. It was interesting to note that both participants were enrolled in two separate colleges and did not have the same advisor. They were also behind one another by two years in classification. Cherise is a sophomore, and Percy is graduating this coming fall. Both participants reported that their advisors were non-Black. Throughout this interview session, the participants did not only report issues with advisors but expressed the manifestation of discrimination by the faculty in the institution.

Faculty Perception and Expectation of Black Students

Busara and I spent a long day analyzing data findings. He informed me that he was leaving on a long journey to Africa. The time had come for him to practice self-meditation and exploration. I knew this time was coming because of all of his recent travel escapades. I knew this would be the beginning of our last conversation and I had to pick his brain. As we sat by the duck pond relaxing in silence, I took the opportunity to speak, hoping he would engage in dialogue. I stated:

> For decades, students of color have reported that faculty members often have
> lower expectations of them in academic settings and because of these
> expectations do not encourage or challenge their learning capacity (Astin et al.,

1972; Chesler, 1996; Kats, 1991; Landsman, 2004; Trujillo, 1986). The testimonies in this section describe similar contextual experiences that support the decades of research conducted by Astin et al. and other sources that I previously mentioned. The State College of the Southwest states on their website they believe that the best educational experience for students is one that is rigorous, challenging, and promotes perseverance through faculty and staff (State College of the Southwest, 2013). This really bothers me as a student, educator, and researcher; it's almost as if I don't know which issue to confront first.

Busara took off his shades, I am guessing so that I could see the seriousness in his face. He stated:

The institution promotes the phantasmal foundation of knowledge concerning the importance of faculty imparting a passion for learning and love for all students. The testimonies of the participants in your research have continually addressed this foundation. You are not dumb, you have learned about instances that even you were oblivious to as a Black woman. What in the hell makes you think that a westernized racist ideologist is paying any attention to the academic and social trials and tribulations these non-white students are facing. If you think they are, you have another thing coming sister girl. You have to open their eyes, remove the blanket. If you don't, you might as well be the oppressor your damn self. How many times do I have to tell you that the problems and issues you have

201

discovered in your research are not just our problem, and I mean Black people. You have to make them everybody's problem! I should push you in this pond. You have to get it together; the information is there for your viewing. It's as if we exist in a racist matrix on this campus; you have already decided whether or not to take the blue or the red pill[14]. You have already digested the red pill, which has removed your blinders. Your reality has become different in the presence of research[15]. Kosik (1976) would define this as your detour, a path which you must take to grasp one cognition of your reality. The complexity of racism as it exists in the social and academic relativities of the State College of the Southwest has emerged in multiple facets. The reality in which you now exist has been crafted through the testimonies of these participants; they have allowed you to develop a phenomenal shape of the racist reality that exists (Kosik, 1976; Lincoln & Denzin, 2000). Your lens has refocused and is seeing things clearer. Use this perception to your advantage.

---

[14] In the movie *The Matrix* (1999), Morpheus tells Neo: "You take the blue pill, the story ends, you wake up in your bed and believe whatever you want to believe. You take the red pill, you stay in Wonderland, and I show you how deep the rabbit hole goes". Busara is referring to this ideology in the context of investigating racism and its impact on Black students in higher education through my research.

[15] Lincoln and Denzin (2000) in "The Discipline and Practice of Qualitative Research" in *The Handbook of Qualitative Research* state that qualitative research in many if not all forms is colonizing because it reports and represents the experience of the "other". In my research, the "other" is represented by Black students and their experiences have created a different meaning in the notion of institutionalized racism. Their testimonies have provided a space for me to step into a different reality, into the domain of racism in education.

Directly after making that statement, Busara walked to the edge of the pond. He turned around and waved at me and told me he would return in time when I really needed him. He assured me that I had it under control. I packed up my blanket, grabbed my purse, and headed back to my home office. I knew it was time to wrap up my next step. I immediately returned to the transcriptions for one last look.

Five was the first to arrive for the interview session this time. He walked into the room and smiled at me from ear to ear. We greeted each other and started a conversation about forthcoming events hosted by the Black Student Association on campus. Midway through our conversation, Percy arrived and TEN followed soon. I looked at the clock – 4:55 pm. All of the participants were about five minutes early. I asked, "Does anyone need to use the restroom or retrieve water before we start?" To my surprise, they all declined. I was ready to begin the interview session, so I turned on the digital voice recorder. My first inquiry referred to either a good or bad experience with faculty here on campus. Five stated that he would like to go first. I gave him the nod of approval, and he began (Field Notes, April 2, 2013):

This professor was a graduate professor. From my perspective, he doesn't like or understand people if they are not Caucasian. I had the honor of taking his class later on in my graduate career. I had to leave the state because of a family emergency. I made him aware of it; he never got back to me. As soon as I got back, I made an appointment to his office to make sure everything was OK and to inform him of my situation. I went to his office, and basically, he got verbally nasty with me during this meeting. I was taking an online class and had never met this professor before. He told me that I was basically irresponsible; I was a lazy person. Previously, I had done everything on time and I still had a good grade in the class. I told him that I do all of my work on time. He said I think you should drop my class, I don't think you're going to make it; I'm going to have to fail you. I couldn't understand this, I told him 70% of my work is done; we are not even at the end of the semester yet and everything we have now is still on the schedule to be handed in, and the deadline is not up. Then I started to hear the same complaints from other non-White students about the same professor. I started to think OK, it's not just me. Some people say he's been here a long time, he getting older, making excuses for his action. Trying to make me understand that this is just the way it is with this professor. I was thinking absolutely not, this is unacceptable. (Five, Graduate, Interview 2, April 2, 2013)

Five had finished speaking and clasped his hands together, then dropping them in his lap. He swayed his leg from side to side. He looked back up and said, "I just could not believe this was happening. I've been an honor roll student throughout my graduate career". Recalling the memory had triggered a small sense of frustration in Five. I waited patiently to see if he had anything else to say. He waved two fingers at me and said, "That's all I have to say about that situation". Percy at this time was ready to share.

She had been watching Five intently throughout his story. I was wondering if she was feeling the same sense of empathy that I had for his struggles. She had her full attention in my direction at this time. She started to speak:

My situation is similar to Five's but in a different context. I have been in situations where I have been accused of plagiarism three times, two in very subtle ways. It doesn't hurt any less each time. The first time I was taking Japanese here years ago. I had a White female professor. This situation is one of the reasons why I will not continue in my Japanese study here at this university. We were doing a photo project, and it was finals week. I was picking up my paper. The assignment was all in Japanese. We had to use certain characters, there were no Romanized characters. So I mean it was good exercise. I did as the professor asked. I'm an over achiever sometimes, so I said to myself I'm going to type this, I'm going to make it neat. I got the paper back, and I looked at and I said "how did I fail this, this is a letter to my friend". She said to me "because you didn't do it, you used a translator". I said to her "are you serious? This must be some kind of joke, who uses translators in their right mind; this is a study that is very important to me". It was a language study. I told her "I did not use a translator. I changed the language settings on my computer and went from there. I downloaded the proper plug in and went from there". Apparently I was too primitive and not smart enough to do this myself, so she made me re-do this paper. I was just like what the hell? My fault for being an overachiever; I mean the insult of her saying that I could not have possibly have known how to do that was crazy. I even tried to show her on her computer, but she would not let me. I think this was because she did not want to look like she had done something wrong. (Percy, Graduate, Interview 2, April 2, 2013)

TEN looked at Percy and shook his head in disgust. He stated:

You think that's bad, let me tell you what happened to me. Now, I don't know if anyone is going to plagiarize a paper on the Non-Nuclear Proliferation Treaty of 1968, who does that? Somehow, I'm not a good writer by any standard, but I understand content, I get the meaning. I brought in a draft to the professor and I was supposed to give it to the graduate assistant. I bought it in but I said look, I know I need to work on the punctuation but all I want to know right now, is if the content is there. Then I started polishing this essay, I took it to the writing center and received a lot of help with my punctuation. The professor, who was White, said I need a meeting with you after I handed in the paper. I'm sitting in a meeting with this professor. The graduate assistant is there and they look at me and he states, "I don't believe you wrote this essay because the difference between the first one and this one is such is stark difference that you couldn't have possibly written this essay". There were two things I realized at this time. The first thing that came to me was I'm that good. The second thing was this is going to affect my grade, this is the final in my 398, class the final course before you can get your BA in history. There is no other course that you can take to get your degree. There was no way for me to prove the negative. So I said ok, well let's have an open discussion and talk about the paper. But then I started to realize how bad this was, the significance of the actual situation. Then I started to realize that plagiarism in academia is sacrilegious. I was distraught, that is the only way to describe it. Even the process of trying to defend yourself is difficult. I didn't understand the whole process of academia at all but I did understand that I had to talk to someone in the department who said I could do an appeal. I was informed by the department that I was the first person ever in the department to do a grade appeal ever because this person tried to fail me. The first one ever and I was like I don't understand how that happened. This guy is really pushing. The process in itself did not allow me to prove myself and that is when you really know your place. It is not objective in anyway, it is subjective, and the people standing there subjecting you to this can determine your future. At the time I was taking an African American history class with the only Black professor in the history department; I think at that time in the whole College of Arts & Sciences. I told him about what was going on and he had already had run-ins with the professor, the one accusing me of plagiarism; he told me that he knew from personal experience how racist this professor was toward non-White students. He then took up my cause. And that was the only reason that I was able to graduate

from the institution and survive because I had someone who already had some

animosity with this professor. I saw this as a true turning point in my life because

I realized that I had enough talent to cause a ruckus. I believed I had enough

talent to conceptualize the Non-Nuclear Proliferation Treaty of 1968.This

moment made me declare that I was going to be the person standing in the

doorway for other people when they have to deal with this crap. (TEN, Graduate,

Interview 2, April 2, 2013)

TEN and Percy both explained a context related to Barton's investigation into

the existence of the academic achievement gap. Professors in educational institutions

have to engage in an examination of the effects of whiteness and its influence on their

educational values and beliefs (Barton, 2004; Foster, 2001; Woodson, 1990). The

research of these scholars explained the position of White privilege and how it

negatively impacts the social and academic actions of White professors towards students

of color. TEN, Percy, and Five share their perceptions of the interactions they had with

professors in an academic setting. Gilbert refers to an academic interaction that speaks

to the same experience as Five but reaches a different outcome of events involving him

and another professor outside of the classroom.

It was my last group of the day. We were wrapping up the section of the session

where I questioned the participants about their academic experiences. Renee and Cherise

208

had both finished sharing their experiences. Gilbert was the last person to share. He had

listened respectfully to the other participants but was very enthusiastic to share his story.

I could tell he was enthusiastic, because when I asked the first question, he said "oh

boy", and clapped his hands together. He asked if I was ready to hear his story. I assured

him that I was ready for him and he went right into telling the group about his

experience. He stated:

> The first thing that comes to my mind when I hear the question is my first
>
> semester at this institution. I took criminal Justice, CJ 101, I can't remember the
>
> professor's name, but the class wasn't so hard. I was kind of busy and I began to
>
> let my grades slip. Me and one of the football players, the starting quarterback,
>
> we helped each other with assignments and sometimes we'd turn them in late
>
> and the football player brought it to my knowledge that the professor was letting
>
> him turn in everything late. He (the quarterback) was a White male, the professor
>
> as well. He was a much older guy though. I asked the teacher for an extension
>
> cause I was flying home and I needed an extension on some homework and he
>
> told me no. He stated that I'm no different from anybody else, you're full of
>
> excuses, I was lazy, and I was like I never even spoke to you before. I had never
>
> met or had a conversation with this man. My roommate was a witness to this at
>
> the time because I actually had to go find this professor in my own time. I found
>
> him in one of his later lectures and waited for his class to end. When I went up to

him and asked for the extension he told me off. In front of a good amount of people, and he was like you know, you're full of excuses. I just let him know, dude, I've never even spoke to you before. I walked off because I was pissed. I said some things under my breath and he was like you want to handle this like men? And I looked back at him, he had taken off his glasses and thrown his hands in the air. I looked back at my roommate and I was like did you hear that? I was like there's no way I'm going to fight a professor in the middle campus. I just walked away; I couldn't believe that this had just happened. I never heard of this professor showing that type of aggression towards any other student. I turned around and he had removed his glasses and was loosening up his tie, it was unbelievable. (Gilbert, Currently Enrolled, March 21, 2013)

The stories shared by Five and Gilbert reveal similarities in their confrontation with White male professors. In both scenarios, the participants explained their reactions to the whole situation. Five stated that he felt like the professor was trying to make him feel inferior and Gilbert said he felt the professor treated him as if he were stupid (Interview, April 2, 2013). The interactions they had are an example of the continuance of racism through microaggressions that are still significantly present in college campuses today (Feagin, 1992; Solórzano et al., 2000; Yosso et al., 1999). In the midst of race-based obstacles, these participants still maintain their faith in education and are extremely focused on the notion of relying on education to give back to their communities.

Conclusion

On the drive home, I thought about my recommendations to the institution. I could not help but think of Audre Lorde's words (2007) *in The Transformation of Silence into Language and Action* (2007):

I was going to die, if not sooner then later, whether or not I had ever spoken myself. My silences had not protected me. Your silences will not protect you. But for every real word spoken, for every attempt I ever made to speak those truths for which I am still seeking. What are the words you do not yet have? What are the tyrannies you swallow day by day and attempt to make your own, until you will sicken and die of them, still in silence? We can learn to speak when we are afraid, in the same way we have learned to work when we are tired. For we have been socialized to respect fear more than our own need for language and definition, and while we sit in silence for that final luxury of fearlessness, the weight of that silence will choke us (p. 41).

When I reached home at night, I went into my room and sat at my desk, consumed by my thoughts. During many moments of silence sitting alone in the small interview room, a million ideas raced through my head. I was overwhelmed by the amount of information I had received through the testimonies. I was even more amazed

211

by the participants' tenacity and perseverance to overcome such circumstances as the ones they had shared. I also felt disappointed in the institution itself and on behalf of student advocacy programs. Even through the session I could not understand how each participant had remained silent about their experiences until my research project offered them a space. I repeated the words of Audre Lorde's *The Transformation of Silence into Language and Action* over and over in my head.

To comprehend the extent of the richness of the experiences described in the participants' testimonies, I incorporated a counter story to portray the ideological constructs of race in education (Lynn & Adams, 2002; Parker & Lynn, 2002). In order to contextualize experiential knowledge and situate the theorizing of race within the context of the university, I walked in tow with multiple critical race theorists and Black feminists throughout this chapter. The attachment of testimony allowed for the crystallization of thematic units as I engaged in data analysis during multiple phases of the study.

Chapter VI

Findings

Primary Findings

Institutionalized Racism

I had finished working on the final analysis of my data. I was logging off my work computer and packing up my materials. As I searched for my keys, I heard a jingling sound in a corner of my office. I turned around to see Busara standing there dangling my keys. He walked around my desk and sat in my chair. He turned the chair to face me and stated:

Humor me for a second about the impact social and academic experiences have on Black students' educational trajectories in higher education institutions. I would also like to know what you have found with regard to racism and its prevalence in the State College of the Southwest. I want to know what you are thinking about these experiences in relation to education and race.

I reflected on Busara's statement for a second and then responded:

The psychologies of our enslaved social constructions are in need of reconstruction (Akbar, 1989). In order to remove these socially conditioned mental chains, I needed the experiences of my participants to develop further understanding of the existence of racism in the systematic structures of the State College of the Southwest. The testimonies reveal the micro and macro levels of

213

racism that manifest in the college's administration, staff, and students [see Chapter 5]. The sociopolitical realities of these participants have been constructed, engulfed, and abused by discrimination and prejudice, these are racist practices. The power and privilege of the academic and social entities at the State College of the Southwest stabilize the political structures that blatantly and subtly discriminate against Black students (Brock, 2005; Watkins, 2001).

Busara nodded his head in agreement. He then made a statement that continually resonates in my mind:

OK, so we know the definition of racism as you referenced Marable (1992) and Audre Lorde (1992) [see Chapter 5]. The form that racism takes within the State College of the Southwest exists in student government, housing administration, staff, academia, and advising to name a few areas that emerged in your research [see Chapter 5]. There is a dissonance between the cultural richness of your participants and the State College of the Southwest (Jagers & Carroll, 2002). The ambivalence of diversity claimed by this institution and the meaning you have stated from a Black feminist and critical race theory perspective requires a space that embraces race, sex, and class and other intersections.

I listened to this statement and replayed it in my head in the moment of silence between Busara and I. I carefully replied:

214

Racism exists in the State College of the Southwest in multiple entities and in the social construction of knowledge and exclusion of experiential knowledge. [see Epistemological Racism, Chapter 5]. TEN and Percy both referred to the absence of a curriculum that engages Black identity, history, and literature [see Chapter 5]. The example of TEN and Percy is one of a multitude of racist actions highlighted in Chapter 5. For example, Five and Percy both talk about the harassment they endured due to Black History Month in front of a student government diversity board that did not see the purpose in bringing Black cultural performers to the institution [see Chapter 5, Racial Microaggressions]. TEN, Percy, Renee, Polo, Five, and Unknown all experienced being on the opposing side of White privilege, stereotypic categorizations, and exclusion at the hands of the same housing director [see Chapter 5, Exclusionary Practices in Campus Housing]. Cornell West (1993) described what the participants' experienced as immoral actions while the institutional responsibility for these immoral practices continues to overlook the very existence of these participants. The predicament these participants have been placed in is one that labels them as the "other" (Brock, 2005).

Busara stated: "But do we all want to be the same?" To which I responded: No, absolutely not. We should not all want to be considered the same as we are all different because of our experiences. That is why an adequate definition of

215

diversity is so important. What is also important is the presence of equitability as this institution should begin to decontextualize and reformulate its practices of diversity. The participants in this study are not the same, but contextually many of their experiences within State College of the Southwest, though disparate and complex, are similar. The process of "othering" is infused with racism, sexism, classism, and many other forms of subordination towards the diverse intersections that Racially Stigmatized Identities possess (Brock, 2005; Solórzano, 1997; 1998). The problem with the "othering" present in State College of the southwest is that it enables discriminatory practices such as the ones faced by these participants by not acknowledging that racism exists within its institutional practices (State College of the Southwest, 2013). Even in silence there is an invisible "violence", a violence of doing nothing that perpetuates the manifestations of racism and other forms of subordination (Bourdieu & Passeron, 2000).

Symbolic Violence

As Busara leaned forward and placed his hand under his chin, he stared at me through his dark brown eyes. I knew that the conversation could turn very serious. I put my bag down on the floor, sat in a chair in front of my desk, since Busara had claimed my work station chair. I ensured I gathered my thoughts before I went into what I knew

216

would be a long process of thought translation. I looked right back, leaned forward, and stated:

Academia prides itself on the symbolism of intelligence, ethics, politics, community, communication, and love (James, 2003). The meaning within such symbolism is violent, in both the pedagogical and political sense (Bourdieu & Passeron, 2000). The participants of this study related issues of racial discrimination attacking their intellectual ability, on campus community, and through their willingness to merely exist in feelings on non-belonging and unwantedness illustrated by the university's staff, students, and administrative bodies [see Chapter 5]. Danie, in particular, stated that "I feel like they [administration and staff] don't want us here [see Chapter 5]". There is a symbolic relation between the agencies using symbolic violence; they are all institutionally and racially related (Bourdieu & Passeron, 2000; Wertsch, 1998). Power and privilege are prominent in each individual experience, even though there are some contextually similar experiences. This happens in every theme throughout this chapter. Whether these racist actions are done in academic or social spaces, my research illustrates that such practices exist. The question I have to ask myself now is where do I go from here with this data I have collected.

Busara smiled from ear to ear. I could sense his approval. He picked up a pencil off my desk and grabbed a sheet from my LaserJet printer. He was drawing some sort of figure. After about five minutes, Busara turned the paper in my direction so that it was no longer upside down–it was just a plain box. Busara smiled at it and asked me, "What do you see here?" I hoped it wasn't some kind of trick question, "I see a box". I looked even closer at the box and noticed it was not a regular box. I answered again, "It is a coffin". Busara said:

Exactly! That is absolutely what you think it is: a coffin. Through this research process a part of you has died, it needed to, in order to bring to life your humanity and a part of your epistemological self (Bahktin, 1991). State College of the Southwest can be a producer of disempowered thoughts that can affect the researcher and those involved in the research. This is the part of you that should have died or is in the process of dying. Your experiences and the participants' dynamic actions directly relate to your internal and research progress – they have started a new beginning (Mills, 2010; Villenas, 2010). You have an eternity to think inside of this box when you are dead. You must continue the reexamination, the changing, and the negotiation of your perceptions, as long as you are living and breathing. I am now going to ask you a question that I want you to really think about before you answer. If things are so discriminatory, or shall we say "bluntly racist" within this institution, why have a third of your

218

participants graduated, a third are currently enrolled past sophomore year, and two of the pushouts returned to the institution?

I reflected on Busara's even-handed question.

The Mythical Understanding in Participant Perseverance and Persistence

I stared at Busara as I reflected on his question, then responded:

I can tell where it is that you are going with this question. Representatives in powerful positions plagued with the ideology of White privilege will read this study and say that these participants are persistent, that the system is set up for everyone to be treated fairly, and succeed as long as they work hard and achieve merit. The modernity of society is optionally conditional in the sense that to achieve such successes, either you modernize along with the normalcies of the dominant majoritarian story or perish (Bauman, 2004). Charles Mills (1997) stated that historically, there has been a racial and social contract that establishes a binary conflict of cultural indifference that enforces majoritarian assimilative practices among non-Whites. Professional discourses in higher education will claim that merit plays a role in the educational status of the three groups in this study. The discourses of White privileged voices will legitimize rhetoric in which opportunity and equality is inevitably gained through hard work, dismissing claims of racism and discrimination in higher education (Bell, 1995).

The institutional presence of modernity is reflective in the consistent low retention and completion rates of not only Black students but students of color (IRPOA, 2008; NCES, 1990, 2000, 2010, 2011). The experiences of these nine participants have not changed; throughout their educational trajectory there is a presence of persistence and perseverance, I do agree [see Chapter 4 profiles]. However, that persistence must not overshadow the presence of racism and discrimination which savagely mars the educational process of Black students in institutions that employ malpractices and misuse terms like diversity and multiculturalism in educational settings. Tinto (1997) stated that persistence is conditioned by the settings in which we work, that is, large residential universities with relatively privileged students who have the luxury to spend time on campus (p. 621). I agree with Tinto's perspective of privilege, but I disagree with his insistence on the conditioning of the individual setting. For example, Polo and his twin brother lived in a park for almost three weeks and during this time, he still remained active in school and on the honor roll [Polo, Pushout, Chapter 4]. TEN grew up with a dope fiend mother and in a very rough neighborhood [TEN, Graduate, Chapter 4]. Then you have Cherise, who is a first-generation college student, whose college counselor was her only informative means into higher education [Cherise, Currently Enrolled, chapter 4]. All of these participants reflected and shared experiences of racism from multiple conditioned entities on campus, both social and academic, that have eventually passed but have stayed with them in some way until this day. It's like in the legal system when a crime is committed and someone is a victim, the system supposedly punishes the guilty party. Racism is a crime, against the humanity of human beings that causes long-term mental and in some cases physical damage (Matsuda, 1993). Yet racism is the hardest crime to prove in a court of law, because it is one that does not befall the privileged White race (Bell, 1987; Crenshaw, 1994).

The racial discrimination these participants faced is just a small representation of the story of perseverance and persistence that does not focus on the racism prevalent in education even prior to entering an institution which has rendered them invisible. The invisibility of these student and their experiences in higher education have neglected their history, interests, and affiliations causing marginality and have been responsible for their oppressive educational experience (Kasworm, 1993; Kasworm et al., 2000; Schlossberg et al., 1989; see Chapter 5). To wrap up, Busara, they are here because they are fighters; but the fight they are battling is one that is often ignored because it is not in the interest of the White privileged majority. These participants have been through academic and social hell and back and have been symbolically violated by the subtlety of discrimination perpetuated by neglect and deficit thinking (Valencia, 1997,

2010). See, the rules of the academic and social game are equal but there is not level playing field (Jost et al., 2005).

Busara stated:

Then what you are saying is that these administrators, staff, and faculty believe in the narrative that education is fair, just, and equal (Jost et al., 2005). To disprove this narrative you have performed research and collected data that says to these administrators and other bodies, *contrary to what you believe or perceive, there is a problem here at this institution and they (administration, staff, students, and faculty) need to fix it!* You believe that these participants are fighting oppression subconsciously and unconsciously for their right for an education in the State College of the Southwest to which they are entitled (Brock, 2005; Freire, 1996).

I responded:

That is exactly what I am trying to say to those multiple entities you named. The reality is that my research alone will not fix institutional racism and discrimination. I believe it was TEN who during the interview eluded that we know racism exists; it's never going to disappear, as a people where should we go from here. Throughout this study, I have named multiple research works that found similar experiences among students, faculty, and staff of color [see References]. There are so many that I cannot name them all. I hope that this

222

institution in particular will read and heed what is happening on the campus of the State College of the Southwest and progress towards an institution that is transformative in thought and deed [see Chapter 7, p. 203].

Busara stood up and pushed in the chair to show me that he was ready to leave. I stood up and pushed my chair back against the wall, grabbed my belongings, and opened the door. I held it open as Busara walked through it; I turned and looked at the drawing of the coffin on my desk. I knew that it was time to end the silence of these participants as well as my own.

Conclusion

The data collected in the study led to the development of recommendations that the researcher submitted to the institution. The overall goal of the research was to provide the institution insight into the perspectives of Black students that could facilitate the transformation of academic and social institutional practices.

The purpose of this research study was to gain a clearer understanding of the relationship that potentially exists between race and education through the academic and social experiences of Black collegiate students. One objective of the research entailed examining the campus climate through the testimonies of Black students at various levels and in different disciplines of education. Throughout the study, the Black student experience was explored to evaluate the phenomena of race, racism, both macro and micro in nature, discrimination, and diversity.

Methods of historical analysis, journaling, interviews, and observations were engaged to collect data. Case study and crystallization were incorporated to analyze and construct thematic codes from the data. The case study approach created spaces throughout the research that allowed access to knowledge regarding each individual participant, group, and the intersections of race and education in the phenomena of the study (Hancock & Algozzine, 2006; Yin, 2003). The method of crystallization allowed the organic emergence of themes from the data collected. The insertion of field notes, participant journals, transcribed interviews, and literature supported the findings expressed throughout the study. The following chapter offers my recommendations in light of these findings.

Chapter VII

Recommendations

A Recommendation for the Study Participants

During the process of data analysis, multiple areas of the testimonies caused great concern for your wellbeing and survival. Throughout the data, there was an expression of loneliness and self-isolation due to the presence of the dominant majority. Do not make excuses for those who have wronged you or allow the "powers that be" any justifications for your marginalization (Crocco & Waite, 2007; Hooks, 1989). You must practice advocacy and persist, no matter what. Paulo Freire (1996) discussed the notion of self-depreciation, deeming it a quality born out of the internalization of the oppressor's opinion. You have fought long and hard to get where you are and there is no place for the feelings of unsuitability and unwelcome in your mental space. At the forefront of discrimination, we have been victims in multiple capacities because of the intersectional differences of race, class, sex, and gender. Yes, we have and continue to be victims of ignorance and fear, but we must not victimize ourselves.

As you sit in your courses as the only Black student, you must advocate against the presence of conventional wisdom. The epistemological position you occupy is one of great significance. Institutional dominance is one that represents a majoritarian culture and mediates actions of discrimination against the culture of the less valued populations of society (Ollman, 1998; Wertsch, 1998). Do not become characters in the assimilated

225

circumstances that exist due to adherence to dominant cultural values. As living and breathing human beings, we need to engage in the practice of capitalizing on our own human capital. The fight against oppression is tough, it is difficult, sickening, but also well overdue, and long; but by no means it is impossible. Institutional discrimination is only a barrier to self-determination. However, if we work together we can create structures, possibilities to overcome such obstacles. I am not recommending that you fight physically, but I am recommending that you fight epistemologically, phenomenologically, holistically, and ontologically. The "epistemological" refers to being aware of the value of the knowledge you possess and its significance, to not only you but to everyone in society (Hill-Collins, 1991, 2000 2001). "Phenomenological" implies knowing that your interpretation and sense of the world are valid, because they form the experiences that define who you are (Fine & Wise, 2010; Lutrell, 2010; Marshall & Rossman, 2011). Throughout our educational experiences we have learned that the social construction of our identity and existence is one that must be renegotiated and reconstructed (Bauman, 1996, 2004). I know that within you there is a sense of doubt, whether or not your experiences matter, you have to make them relevant. Holistically, you have to embrace the interconnectedness of social factors that have overtime conditioned many of us into believing we are inferior (Hooks, 1994; Marshall & Rossman, 2011). Inferiority is a part of structural and institutional systems that disempower one's being (Giroux, 1997; Kincheloe, 2004; McClaren, 2000); it forms an equation of lies, discrimination, and hate that have existed historically and now have evolved to manifest in our lives (Bell, 1992; Hooks& West, 1991). Ontologically, you have to recognize that your differences do not form the issue; how a dominant majority views our diversity and then treats us based on stereotypical notions historically constructed is the problem (Aronson & Steele, 1997; Steele, 1992).

My goal here is not to scold you as a mother does to a child or shame you. My goal is to encourage, one advocate to another, and to motivate potential advocates to take a stand against historical practices of discrimination that still prevail in this nation and are manifesting in our higher education institutions. The building of student, faculty, and administrative coalitions is the initial step to this process.

To Academia and Administration of State College of the Southwest: The Reconstruction of Policy, Procedures, in Institutional Academic and Social Practices

Racial discrimination is a reality in your institution. The certainty of evidence is formed by the testimony of these nine study participants [see Chapter 5]. Denying or ignoring racism or its existence is an utter injustice to your students of color and a perpetuation of White supremacy and privilege (Bell, 1995; Pellar, 1995). Reformation of your policies and practices to ensure equity for all students and the meaning of diversity in your institution entail the following:

- In your strategic visions, when you create strategies to recruit more diverse faculty, that is not enough (State College of the Southwest, 2013). You must redefine and implement multicultural goals to create real diversity and promote awareness through more university entities than faculty alone (Bell, 1995).

- Overcoming the racist practices at the institutional level requires a substantial amount of social and academic resources and administrative energy by transforming the appropriation of funding to recruit more students of color as well as staff and the development of cultural programs (Peller, 1995).

- Embracing on-campus and off-campus communities of color in all academic disciplines. Involvement in the funds of experiential knowledge means inclusion of the Black community on campus. This community currently faces rejection, racial profiling, and exclusion in your classrooms, in your student government, and positioning their faces through media outlets is an insult to their existence, cultural capital, and ability (Allen, 1970; Moll et al., 2005; Peller, 1995; State College of the Southwest, 2013).

The indestructible permanence of racism prevails in our institutions because you have ignored the frequent occurrence of discrimination, there are eyes that are blind and eyes that have been shut, the wool has been pulled over to block out the truth, and the inability to recognize and confront discriminatory acts (Bell, 1992; Brock, 2005; Du Bois, 1903; King, 1995; Lorde, 1996). The information provided through the testimonies and throughout these recommendations is not some new revelation; Blacks have existed in a subordinate status within your institution since the graduation of the first Black female graduate a century ago (State College of the Southwest, 2013). The color barriers are long standing, no less real or oppressive, and the only difference is the visibility of your discriminatory ways has changed (Bell, 1995). The learning mechanism and strategic visions meant to embrace diversity are plagued with conventional wisdom and reek of a westernized political ambiguity towards the actual meaning of diversity (Ani, 1994; Asante, 1991; Matsuda, 1993). To embrace diversity, there is a need to recognize experiential knowledge as legitimate in academia, especially the classroom and administrative offices.

The laws, policies, and procedures enable an educational contradiction of equality and equity and continue the promotion of racism by imposing hegemonic goals, objectives, and outcomes in higher education (Bell, 1992; Matsuda, 1993). The ideology that equality and diversity now exist at State College of the Southwest is endorsed by overarching agendas that forefront accomplishments such as the graduation of the first Black woman in higher education in the early 20th century (State College of the Southwest, 2013). The semi-factual events such as this must allow the counter story that remains untold. This woman's learning opportunity was not the same as other students; she remained in the hallway during instruction and was unable to join her non-Black colleagues in the classroom (Speech, 2011). The feeling of unworthiness caused by being unable to sit at the table with her colleagues is still present among students in your institution; it is mentioned in the testimonies.

229

These nine participants have been victims of macro and micro racist acts on multiple occasions in your institution at the hands of a "diverse" number of entities (State College of the Southwest, 2013). These human beings have been riddled with essentialist actions that have justified acts of exclusion and discrimination. Essentializing a group of people can lead to their oppression and marginalization because it negatively impacts their intellectual progression and motivation for learning (Aronson & Steele, 1997; Delgado & Stefanic, 2001; Steele, 2009).To achieve actual progression, you should not only read this dissertation, and similar works, critically and with an open mind, similar works, but continue to research existing conditions of domination in your institution. The initial prescription I am providing will not cure or rid your systems overnight – it will take time, commitment, and an unbending responsibility to respond to overt and covert practices of oppression that have been institutionalized.

Acknowledging the Meaning of Diversity and the Evolution of Racism

In 2006, Gloria Ladson-Billings delivered a presidential address at AERA where she testified to the educational debt of our nation and higher educational institutions. Ladson-Billings stated that the term achievement gap in Google search engine produced 11 million citations; today, seven years later, that number has risen to 21,900,000. I am giving this example because I hope to provide insight into the gaps that exist within our post-secondary education system and how they have evolved overtime. The achievement

230

gap in higher education is a product of institutionalized discrimination and systematic racism that exists within our higher educational institutions (Apple, 2000; Hill-Collins 2001; Hooks, 1994; Pinar, 2005; Valencia, 1997, 2010). Some would like to believe that racism no longer exists or at least not within our institutions. I was recently informed by a presidential candidate in our institution, who, when asked what he would do to combat racism responded: "racism does not exist at State College of the Southwest". Either this person has blinders on or a blanket has been pulled over his eyes or he is just ignorant about the existence of institutionalized racism due to his position and White privilege. There is great concern regarding the wellbeing and survival of diverse populations in reference to educational outcomes, especially considering departments of ethnic studies that have helped many Black students during our educational trajectory. "Diversity" has become a safe and convenient word for education, misused and abused, now marketable, employed to enhance the production of the White majority. Diversity, as defined by some Black feminist and critical race scholars, relates to race, class, gender, and other forms of discrimination. To adequately define diversity, an examination of race, class, and gender in accordance with the assessment of education, including academic and social environments, requires a collaboration of multicultural perspectives (Collins & Andersen, 2000; Banks, 2001; Sleeter, 2000). Though our educational institutions have represented diversity as a mix of races working collaboratively in the classroom, there are gaps, especially untold stories excluded in terms of the representation of diversity.

231

The untold stories could serve as a knowledge source for creating liberatory policies, procedures, and academic practices. Throughout my time here at State College of the Southwest, I noticed an atmosphere representative of diversity. However, that diversity is overshadowed by a subtle presence of isolation, discrimination, and marginalization that creates loneliness and self-isolation, due to the presence of a dominant majority that excludes the cultural wealth and richness possessed by students, staff, and faculty of color. I am not saying we are not allowed the opportunity to sit at the round table during discussions, but the voices we represent are drowned out by what are considered much more worthy and important causes.

We have referred to the Civil Rights era as a time of progress and great measures. I am thankful for the symbolic and needed efforts, especially on behalf of those of my race who marched, protested, and fought both physically and strategically to improve the current economic and social conditions that existed at the time. Racism itself has changed form; it has manifested in multiple silhouettes and is evolving through systematic practices (Bell, 1995). As I reflect on the concept of racism, I think about how the signs have changed. Notice that I said signs and not times. In 2004, my family drove to New Mexico to pick me up after graduation; as we traveled along Interstate 54 East to head back home, I remember stopping to eat at a small dinner in Amarillo, Texas. The sign on the door did not read, "Whites only," but it did read "gone to a hanging". I want you to understand that the sign didn't say blatantly that we were not allowed to eat at the restaurant, but what it did was state the consequences for our actions if we felt that we were entitled to sit in that restaurant. In that moment, I had to reflect on how far we had progressed as a society and yet how stationary we remain. As I stood there and read this sign, reflecting on the meaning, I turned around and noticed that the rest of my family had immediately returned to the car. I had never seen my step-father and mother move so fast, but I also realized they grew up in a much different time. The message that we received in that moment, whether it had been in the 1960's or in the year 2004, was that "your kind is not welcomed". And the rest of the 12 hour trip home the message we individually received was the same, but our interpretation of what should be done was different. Now, what does this have to do with education, a question that some of you might be asking yourselves.

I have for the past four years, along with scholars all across the world, been conducting and studying research regarding the Black student experience in higher education; the message that my family and I received in Amarillo Texas is one that we as Black students and Racially Stigmatized Identities have been receiving, of not being welcome or "knowing one's place" within our educational institutions. Whether it is relayed to our student organizations, during the process of tenure for faculty of color, or as an educator or student in the classroom, hearing the biases from racial micro and macro aggressions from our peers and colleagues. Racism exists at two levels, the micro and macro. I bring up racism because it is one of the most denied forms of intersectional

233

subordination when it comes to admitting its existence (Bell, 1987, 1992; Hooks, 1981; Collins & Andersen, 2001; Lorde, 1991; Marable, 1991). Racism is embedded in the process by which we are educated at the primary, secondary, and post-secondary levels and continues to evolve in education. In the last couple of months at State College of the Southwest, there have been acts of racism – tagging posters about the first Black female student body president with racial slurs. Similar incidents at two separate colleges also happened during the time of this study, at Oberlin College and the University of Mississippi, where posters of president Obama were burned and racial slurs were prominently yelled. On April 30, 2013, I received a call from a Black male student whom I mentor. He said that he needed to speak with me regarding an incident that took place at the community college partnered with our campus. This student was verbally attacked by an older White male due to his race during a presentation in his communications course. This man spoke of how African Americans are unproductive, hot tempered, and how he would never hire Black people to work for him due to these reasons. The situation spun out of control and turned into a very aggressive argument between the two as no one in the class took the time to stand up for the student; they waited until after class to speak with him. Security was called, and the Black student was handcuffed. I mention these things because in order to first combat an issue, you must acknowledge that it exists. Robin Barnes(1991) stated that Racially Stigmatized

Identities have to constantly fight for their rights that other privileged White people feel entitled to, whether in education or other institutions.

In the 1960's, the Civil Rights campaign fought against racism and its existence and during that time; educational research continued the manifestation of a deficit lens and incomplete attributors to the lack of success among African Americans in our educational system. Reports all through history have argued that a cultural deficit existed among Black students in the educational system by stating that Black students have a lack of familial support, that language, the placement of schools and so on were factors that contributed to the achievement gaps in education (DuBois, 1903; Hernstein & Murray, 1996; Ladson-Billings, 2006; Woodson, 1930). As a researcher in making, I stand here before you as a product of a single parent home, where there were times with no electricity. On numerous occasions, I carried water in a bucket from the house next door in which my siblings and I bathed. My family and I moved from house to house a total of 17 times from the time I was in kindergarten to a senior in high school. Many of the students that I work with today at State College of the Southwest come from backgrounds with stories of various struggles, from extreme conditions of poverty and enrollment in high-poverty educational institutions; yet, we are here today. But within the lines of those struggles there is a story of persistence, a cultural richness, a motivation that at times can go unnoticed and overlooked. As fortunate as we are to have overcome such obstacles, we have to continue to pave those pathways to create opportunities we wish we had, for others as so many have done for us. There is nothing in this world that is more disappointing than listening to students of color say that they just want to live comfortably in life. Well, the notion of comfort cannot be one that is founded strictly on financial capability, because if you were a millionaire living in Mississippi, or attending Oberlin College or a victim of the 250,000 hate crimes that take place on a yearly basis in this country (FBI database, 2013), are you still able to live comfortably?

Absolutely not! So then the question becomes even though we have been victims of such subtle and heinous discriminatory acts, where do we sit or stand during trying times. Do we take a back seat, sit at the front, or begin to drive the bus that advocates for our purpose and right to receive equitably and socially just treatment in a country that we helped build and have taken our place as leaders and role models?

Recommendations of Research Findings

During the interview session, TEN asked the question: "What are higher educational institutions really doing to combat racism on campus?" I continually reflected on this question throughout the process of data analysis. A commonality that appeared between all three groups in my collective case study caused a redirection of this question. The question that actually surfaced after reviewing participant testimony was "Why are the socially just responsibilities of higher educational institutions almost non-existent as micro and macro levels of racism exist in the campus climate?" A

236

second question derived during my reflection was as follows: "What are students doing to fight back against the power and privilege of administrative bodies in higher education?

The primary finding that emerged from the data centered on the presence of racial microaggressions by multiple entities on campus. The following recommendations are based on the crystallized themes in Chapter Five.

An Institution-Wide Primary Recommendation: Improving the Incorporation of Diversity and Diverse Practices

The Inclusion of Cultural Discourses

When racial microaggressions happen, university administration, faculty, student body, and staff must develop a critical understanding of race by examining the accessibility of education, student persistence, and the road to graduation of Black students (Carroll, 1998; Hurtado, 1992; Allen, 1999). The defining of student success calls for a reevaluation and restructuring through the examination of the cultural, historical, racial, and social character of students' intersectional capital. In order to adequately assess student achievement, the institution must develop a strategy to unmask the two dimensional hegemonic structures within academia, administration, and social settings that illustrate the majoritarian culture versus "the other currently in place within academic and social systems.

In my search of the word diversity in university reports, on websites and within admission pamphlets, I could not find an actual definition of the term by the institution. Conversely, what I did find representing the word diversity was a mainstream common sense term representing the interest of the White majority. For example, multiple departments and colleges within the institution refer to diversity in their strategic visions (State College of the Southwest, 2013). The presence of diversity is not the problem; it is in the practice of the idea of diversity where meaning is nullified. The mention of diversity is frequent in brochures containing pictures of students from multiple backgrounds or pictures of staff and students from various racial backgrounds doing research, teaching courses, all based on physical appearance across the campus. The practice of diversity is fallacious without an understanding of its meaning and context, which can occur in multiple capacities. Such collaborative perspectives must include the multicultural presence of an actual student body that represents the cultural wealth that Racially Stigmatized Identities possess. The inclusion of cultural discourses of Racially Stigmatized Identities is desperately needed at multiple institutional levels to exhibit the impact of the social constructs of diversity in the presence of intersections such as race and education. The power and privilege of the majoritarian story has never been and is no longer adequate in assessing the potential of students of color in education (Brock, 2005; Sleeter, 2001, 2005; Steele, 2009; Woodson, 1930). Education needs more professors, administrators, and staff who are not only aware but knowledgeable of the

238

cultural richness professors, students, administrators, and staff of color contribute to higher education (Sleeter, 2001).

Reconstructing and Defining Diversity

The conditions in which students are placed in the institution such as on campus housing, classrooms, admissions, security, and student government calls for an equitable and socially just existence. In order to achieve this, the very character of the foundations that constitute these socio-educational settings require reconstituting the actual values the institution has in place through the assessment of historical, current, and future student experiences. Research performed by Allen et al. (1991) and Carroll (1998) has proven that an unsupportive campus climate is related to the underachievement and incompletion rate of Black students. Tinto (1997) stated that a number of researchers have focused on the role of pedagogy (e.g., Karplus, 1974; Lawson & Snitgen, 1982; McMillan, 1987) and, in turn, curriculum (e.g., Dressel & May- hew, 1954; Forrest, 1982) and classroom activities (e.g., Volkwein et al., 1986) as predictors of student learning (p. 601).To practice equitable and socially just sustainment of students of color, the campus climate of the State College of the Southwest has to be more supportive of diversity. My recommendations for reconstructing and redefining diversity are supported by the theoretical frameworks of Black feminism, critical race theory, and multiculturalism. According to Astin (1993), Banks (2005), Hooks, (1994), Delgado Bernal and Villalpando (2002), Ladson-Billings (1992, 2006) Sleeter (2005), Tinto

(1993) (2003), and Yosso(2005), to provide a diversity friendly institution, the State

College of the Southwest must practice the following:

- Exclude the one diversity or multicultural course fix-it principle to solve the understanding of diversity (Tinto, 1993, 2003);

- Institute curriculum and professional development that incorporates the complexity of language, race, ethnicity, class, and sex [among other intersections] that is consistent and widely offered in an array of departments across all colleges;

- Institute curriculum and professional development that explains that knowledge is socially constructed and the biases created from the ideologies of a western and White dominant philosophy are responsible for an economic, political, and cultural system that is discriminatory against non-White people;

- In your strategic visions, you have stated that the recruitment of diverse faculty is imminent across the institution (State College of the Southwest, 2013). Nine academic departments do not have any faculty of color (State College of the Southwest, 2013). Over 60% of faculty members within the institution have felt discriminated against on the basis of race and gender (IRPOA, 2013). I am recommending the continued recruitment and retention of faculty of color because research shows that teachers of color have more success when educating students of color (Ladson-Billings, 1998; Sleeter, 2005).

Recognizing the critical importance of such faculty involves the legitimizing of experiential knowledge and equitable inclusion and consideration in powerful and privilege administrative positions (Delgado-Bernal & Villalpando, 2001);

- The College State of the Southwest must institute across the board the exercising of cross-cultural group memberships and equitable treatment during the process of creating those relationships. In Chapter 5, participants explained the discriminatory practices of the student government's diversity board during a proposal review for Black history month. Student organizations need to embrace diversity as well and allow the equitable treatment of students representing multicultural groups. Faculty advisors as well as administrators need to develop a policy that encourages cross-cultural group collaborations that are equitable and socially just;

- Faculty in multiple disciplines must also include multicultural teaching and learning practices to develop, assess, and embrace complex cognitive abilities; this requires a development and understanding of student background (King, 1991; Moll, et al., 2005), a commitment to social justice teaching practices, (Su, 1996, 1997), the development of an epistemological base that encompasses culturally diverse communities and critical pedagogies (Hooks, 1994; Moll et al., 2005).

- Faculty, staff, teachers, and administration should learn about stereotyping and other related biases that have negative effects on racial and ethnic relations (Banks, 2005).

Accomplishing diversity and multiculturalism will not be an easy task, but it is possible. It will take time to develop and even more time to assess. State College of the Southwest already has goals to achieve diversity in its strategic vision and plans. Work towards these goals now and adhere to these recommendations with an open mind and the willingness to progress.

Inclusive Approaches of Campus Housing and Student Government

The State College of the Southwest cornerstones its campus climates through social exclusionary practices that marginalize and isolate Black students. Tinto (2002) stated that the educational conditions within institutions must promote educational success of all and not just some students. In the State College of the Southwest, student government committees and campus housing staff and administrators are currently engaging in discriminatory practices [see Chapter 5]. The racially discriminatory actions reported by the participants by the housing and government entities are a reality for a majority of these participants.

Academic Discrimination

Reconstructing Knowledge

Academic integration is a condition for student success (Astin, 1993, 1997, Tinto, 1993, 2003). In order to unlearn epistemological racism, the institutional governing bodies must promote the liberation of diverse student populations, in particular students of color. Beginning the process of liberation and fortifying its existence calls for theorizing and analyzing the potential epistemological presence of a diverse student population (Maddox & Solórzano, 2002; Ladson-Billings, 1995, 1998). The current foundation of institutional system is foundationally privileged which causes a difficulty in not only the acknowledgement of racial differences, but in the treatment. The privileged foundations that exist within higher education have historically made the knowledge of Racially Stigmatized Identities irrelevant through the fallacious ideology of cultural depravity that supposedly exists within communities of color (Persell, 1977; Semali & Kincheloe, 1999; Valencia & Solórzano, 1997). Currently, the college climate has created an adversarial stance in the embracement of race through the denial of the importance of experiential knowledge; this is preventing the right to an equitable educational experience for Black students.

Black students are agents in the development of their own knowledge. The agency they possess is important to the growth and development of the institution, especially during a transformative time of need. The initiation of social justice and

243

democracy cannot solely rely on the efforts of the administration of the College. Ethnic programs, faculty, community leaders and organizations, and students have to develop multiple courses of action to confront issues of discrimination. By limiting the potential of advocacy that a collaboration of such forces collectively encompass is an injustice to your own potential positions of power. Students must become advocates and that should not be limited to self-advocating; you have to work together with your peers and colleagues to achieve greater results.

The incorporation of more *multicultural on campus and off campus based research* is needed to provide an adequate understanding of the multicultural capital and communal cultural wealth that currently exists on the State College of the Southwest's campus. To understand the salient issues that student communities of color face on campus, there is a definite need for multiple research approaches whether empirical, ethnographic, and so on. Processes that involve the collection and incorporation of stories are critical components in the construction of knowledge (Hooks, 1993; McAllister & Irvine, 2000; Merriam 1998).

Academic support is a condition necessary for the continuation of students in higher education (Tinto, 2003). To ensure a democratic and socially just process of academic advising, advisors need to maintain an adequate time of availability for these students. The caseload for academic advisors requires equitable distribution and an adequate assessment of student potential and capability, one that is inclusive of student perspective. The offices of academic advising require professional development and consistency.

Instilling Cohesive Cultural Forces to Improve Retention

As early as the 1960's, the State College of the Southwest as well as a majority of institutions in the United States maintained a high attrition rate for students of color(IROPA, 2008; NCES, 1980; 1990; 2000; 2010). In order to promote student success, universities across the nation have invested money in resources to formulate a strategy to improve the retention rates of students of color (Kuh, 2003; Tinto, 1994, 2003). Institutions that want to improve in the area of retention have to wake upto the need for transformative practices in their college climate. The creation of spaces that discuss the impact of race and racism within a college setting in and outside the classroom are not enough, they are a beginning to a means that is far from ending. To critically evaluate the structural and cultural aspects of education, there is a need for socially just action by the faculty, students and administrators, to confront the subordinate and dominant racial positions strategically in place. The themes in this study are not new findings; what makes these findings new is that they were a result of this study. Unfortunately, the findings are a mirror representation of existing practices uncovered through decades of research (Allen, 1984; DuBois, 1903; Hooks, 1991; Kushner, 1980; Woodson, 1933).

In various departments within the State College of the Southwest, there is a common goal set throughout, starting in 2012, to increase the percentage of faculty of color in academia. Growing trends in education have estimated that by the year 2023, Racially Stigmatized Identities will represent over 50% of students enrolled in educational institutions. Academic programs now have the responsibility of making the educational contributions of Racially Stigmatized Identities relevant in primary, secondary, and post-secondary levels of education. The intellectual discourse in academia requires a perspective to initiate the broadening and usurpation of privileged lenses and entitlement present in the teaching practice of White faculty. As the number of faculty and students of color increases in higher education, so should collaborations and coalitions of social justice, multiculturalism, and democratic perspectives. Administrators must not only bring to the table faculty and students of color, but you have to listen, respect, and make sure that you understand their experiences. Understanding should result in the use of those experiences as foundations for academic and social program implementation.

Reevaluating the Complexity of Student Engagement

Student involvement in learning is important to the classroom. Engaging students in their learning process will promote student success. Racially Stigmatized Identities bring a cultural richness into the learning environment beneficial to all teachers and learners (Sleeter, 2001, 2004, 2005). Faculty in higher education should

246

enhance learning to promote the success of all of their classroom students and not just some. Student persistence and involvement in learning environments with their peers show a greater level of intellectual development. Therefore, the opportunity to engage in such a collaborative learning process should be made possible in spaces where learning can take place. Learning is a key process in student success. A student who is engaged is a student who is learning, and students who learn are more likely to remain and complete their education (Tinto, 1997, 2003).

Epilogue

Limitations of the Study

One limitation of the study is that as the researcher, I selected students I was familiar with due to my work as a student mentor in the department that provided the selection sample. The time frame for conducting data collection and analysis data was another limitation. After a five month, 15-member Institutional Review Board committee approval process, the research proposal was finally granted approved. The interviews and observations took place over the time frame of eight weeks. Data analysis took another four weeks.

Undergoing Transformation

One essential goal throughout the collection, analysis, and reporting of the research data was to remain true to the testimonies of the participants. As the primary researcher, one of my primary goals during the data analysis of the study was not to speak for the participants, and only serve as a median (Fine & Weis, 2010; Villenas, 2010), to speak on their behalf; to perceive it any other way would have been a malevolent act. My position was going to be as a fool with knowledge or a researcher full of knowledge. The difference between those two concepts is substantial. I had the opportunity to engage myself in the research and believe that I knew these participants and had lived their stories, or I could travel the path of unknowing and humility and allow these participants to construct the story and become the teachers and storytellers. The process of remaining loyal to participants' experiences, shared through their words, was supported by the objective to allow the participants to become agents in the purpose of the research and the possibility of advocating for a more socially just and democratic higher education system. In order to remain dedicated to the achievement of this goal, my efforts required diligent and ethical acts. The incorporation of the counter story was academically necessary when confronting the continual challenge of conventional wisdom in relation to the intermingling of intersectional discriminatory practices in higher education. Counter story allowed a narrative reflective of the multiple consciousness (Du Bois, 1903, 1994), wherein I could critically clarify alternative thoughts and reflections while staying true to the testimonies of the participants.

A reflective surfacing of my personal experiences in relation to the phenomena, as the primary researcher, occurred on numerous occasions, allowing a reconstruction of "self" (Bahktin, 1991).Throughout this research process, my identity was changing. I had to rethink the colonized meaning of my identity while I myself had become a *replica* of the colonizer during my research of the "other" (Brock; 2005; Villenas, 2010).The richness and depth in participant stories enabled me in the position of the researcher to reconsider critically the phenomena under investigation while developing an additional lens, one that instigated the notion of humanity, and what it meant to be human while fighting multiple dehumanizing acts and thoughts. To acquire a new lens called for the integration of experiential knowledge, one that carried responsibilities and called critical readjustments stemming from constant reflections, practicing humility. Humility prevailed during numerous parts of the research process, especially during the period of data analysis and collection. Analyzing the shared experiences of each participant opened a space that involved the manifestations of pain, joy, and wanted needs of advocacy within myself as the primary privileged researcher.

One privilege which surfaced during the recognition of my position as the primary researcher meant acknowledging that I sat in the position of the final translator of my participant's stories. I had to remember that each individual story, though united during the crystallization of the data, possessed its own value, integrity, and meaning. Constant critique of my own self critiques constructed complexities developed through repeated analysis of field notes, interviews, and journal reflections. I was no stranger to my conflicting contradictions, as a Black woman who encountered issues of racism and discrimination, I made assumptions regarding the participants' experiences. I believed that these participants had experienced the same incidents, and although they did on many accounts experience racism, in some cases it was not at all similar to my own personal racist encounters. I evaluated these contradictions by discussions with my colleagues, reading multiple works of literature, and listening to the experiences of the participants; these were my outlets, another set of eyes and ears during these self-critiques.

My methods were constructed on the premise of investigating the social and academic change for Black students. The purpose of the findings from the data in the study was to take the multiple experiences of Black students in post-secondary educational institutions and transform institutional policies and academic and social practices to help improve their graduation rates and the educational experience of Black students. In the end, my blackness holds an important position in the construction of my identity; it is heavily connected to the research process, to my subjective being. I carry my subjectivity in a bagpacked tightly with marginalization, complicity, resentment, and multiple struggles in relation to my educational experiences. Listening to and sharing the experiences of my participants opened a space for the disassociation of my realizations in comparison to theirs. The realization that a counterpoise existed in the experiences of the participants with regard to my own caused a self-confrontation. The belief that our oppressions were similar did not prove incorrect in my research, but in discovering this

concept, I had to acknowledge a difference in the context of our oppressions.

References

Adelman, L. (Director). (2003). *Race:The story we tell* [Motion Picture].

Allen, W. R. (1992). The color of success: African American college student outcomes at predominantely White and Historically Black public colleges and Universities. *Harvard Educational Review*, 26–44.

Allen, W. R., & Haniff, N. Z. (1991). Race, gender, and academic performances in U.S. higher education. In W. R. Allen, E. G. Epps, & N. Z. Haniff (eds.), *College in Black and White: African American students in predominantly White and historically Black public universities* (pp. 95–105). State University of New York Press.

Alon, S. & Tienda, M. (2005). Assessing the "mismatch" hypothesis: Differences in college graduation rates by institutional selectivity. *Sociology of Education, 78,* 294–315.

Anderson, G. (1989). Critical ethongraphy in education: Origins, current status, and new directions. *Review of Educational Research*, 249–270.

Anderson, G., & Herr, K. (1993). The micropolitics of student voices:Moving from diversity of voices in schools. In C. Marshall, *The new politics of gender and race* (pp. 58–68). Falmer Press.

Andersen, M. L., & Collins, P. H. (2004). *Race class and gender* (5th ed.). Wadsworth/Thomson Learning.

Anderson, J. (1988). *The education of Blacks in the south, 1860-1935.* University of

    North Carolina Press.

Ani, M. (1994*). Yurugu: An African-centered critique of European cultural thought and*

    behavior. Africa Free World Press.

Anyon, J. (2005). *Radical possibilities. Public policy, urban education, and a new social*

    movement. Routledge.

Apple, M. (1985). *Education and power.* Routledge.

Apple, M. (1990). *Ideology and curriculum* (2nd ed.). Routledge.

Apple, M. (1992). Text and cultural politics. *Educational Researcher, 21*(7), 4–19.

Apple, M., & Beyer, L. (1998).Values and politics in the curriculum. In L. Beyer & M.

    Apple, *The curriculum: Problems, politics, and possibilities*, 3–16. New York

    Press.

Apple, M. (2000). Can critical pedagogies interrupt rightist policies? *Educational*

    Theory, 50(2), 229–254.

Aronson, J., & Inzlicht, M. (2004). The ups and downs of attributional ambiguity:

    Stereotype vulnerability and the academic self-knowledge of African American

    college students. *Psychological Science, 15*, 829–836

Asante, M. K. (1991). The Afrocentric idea in education. *Journal of Negro Education,*

    60, 170–179.

Astin, A. W. (1968). Undergraduate achievement and institutional excellence. *Science*, (161), 661–688.

Astin, A. W. (1971). *College impact on student attitudes and behavior*. Paper presented at the Annual Meeting of the American Educational Research Association, New York.

Astin, A. W. (1982). *Minorities in American higher education: Recent trends, Current prospect, and recommendations*. Jossey-Bass.

Astin, A.W. (1982). *What matters in college? Four critical years revisited*. Jossey-Bass.

Atlas, R. S., & Pelpers, D. J. (1998). Observations of bullying in the classroom. *The Journal of Educational Research*, 86–99.

Ayers, M. Quinn, T., & Stovall, D. (2009).Handbook of social justice in education. Routledge.

Baldwin, J. (1985). *The price of the ticket*. St. Martin's Press.

Banks, J. (1995). The historical reconstruction of knowledge about race: Implications for transformative teaching. *Educational Researcher*, *24*, 15–25.

Barnes, R. (1990). Colloquy: Race consciousness: The thematic content of racial distinctiveness in critical race scholarship. *Harvard Law Review*, *103*(1864).

Bauman, Z. (2004). *Wasted lives. Modernity and its outcasts*. Polity Press.

Bell, D. (1992). *Faces at the bottom of the well*. Basic Books.

Bell, B., Gaventa, J., & Peters, J. (1990). *We* make *the road by walking. Conversations of education and social change.* Myles Horton and Paulo Freire. Temple University Press.

Beverly, J. (2000). Testimonio, subalternity, and narrative inquiry. In N. K. Denzin & Y. S. Lincoln (2000). *Handbook of Qualitative Research* (pp. 555–565). Sage Publications.

Blauner, R. (1972). *Racial oppression in America.* Harper and Row.

Boske, C. A. (2010). I wonder if they had ever seen a Black man before? Grappling with issues of race and racism in our own backyard. *Journal of Research on Leadership Education*, (7), 248–275.

Bourdieu, P., &Passeron, J. C. (2000). *Reproduction in education society and culture.* Sage Publications.

Brock, R. (2005). *Sister talk*. Peter Lang.

Carey, K. (2005). One step from the finish line: Higher college graduation rates are within our reach. *The Education Trust*. Retrieved from http://www2.edtrust.org/NR/rdonlyres/highered.pdf

Cokley, K. (2000). An investigation of academic self-concept and its relationship to academic achievement in African American college students. *Journal of Black Psychology, 26*(2), 148–164.

Chávez, R. C., Belkin, L. D., Hornback, J. G., & Adams, A. K. (1991). Dropping out of
school: Issues affecting culturally, ethnically, and linguistically distinct student
groups. *The Jornal of Educational Issues of Language Minority Students*, 1–13.

Collins, P. H. (1989). The social construction of Black feminist thought. *Signs*, *14*(4),
7745–7773. Retrieved from www.jstor.org/stable/3174683

Collins, P. H. (1998). It's all in the family: Intersections of gender, race, and nation.
Hypatia, *13*(3), 62–80.

Collins, P. H. (2000). Black feminist thought in a matrix of domination. In P. H. Collins,
*Black feminist thought:Knowledge, consciousness, and the politics of
empowerment* (2nd ed.) (pp. 221–238). Routledge.

Crenshaw, K. W. (2002). The first decade: Critical reflections, or "a foot in the closing
door". *UCLA Review*, *49*(1343), 1343–1372.

Croco, M.S., & Waite, C. L. (2007). Education and marginality: Race and gender in
higher education, 1940-1955. *47*(1), 70–91.

Cross, T., & Slater, R. (2000). The alarming decline in the academic performance of
African-American men. *The Journal of Blacks in Higher Education*, *27*, 82–87.

Cross, T., & Slater, R. (2001). The troublesome decline in African-American college
student graduation rates. *The Journal of Blacks in Higher Education*, *33*, 102–
109.

Cullen, J. (2004). *The American dream: Ashort history of an idea that shaped a nation.* Oxford University Press.

Davis, J. E. (1994). College in Black and White: Campus environment and academic achievement of African American males. *Journal of Negro Education,63*, 620–633.

DeCuir, J. T., & Dixson, A. D. (2004). "So when it comes out, they aren't that surprised that it is there": Using critical race theory as a tool of analysis of race and racism. *Educational Researcher*, 26–41.

De'Souza, D. (1991). *Illiberal education: The politics of race and sex on campus.* Free Press.

Delgado, R., & Stefanic, J. (2001). *Critical race theory. An introduction.* New York University Press.

Dessel, A. (2010). Prejudice in schools: Promotion of an inclusive culture and climate. *Education and Urban Society*, 407–429.

DuBois, W. E. B. (1994). *The sous of Black folk.* Dover Publications.

Feagin, J. (1977). Indirect institutionalized discrimination. *American Political Quarterly*, (5), 177–200.

Feagin, J., & Feagin, C. B. (1978). *Discrimination American style.* Prentice-Hall.

Feagin, J.,& Eckberg, D. (1980). Discrimination: Motivation, action, and context. *Annual Review of Sociology*, (6), 1–20.

Feagin, J., & Sikes, M. P. (1995). How Black students cope with racism on White campuses. *The Journal of Blacks in Higher Education*, (8), 91–97.

Fine, M. (1991). *Framing dropouts: Notes on the politics of urban highschool.* State University of New York Press.

Fine, M., & Rosenberg, P. (1983). Dropping out of high school: The ideology of school and work. *Standard Education Almanac*, 450–464.

Fredua-Kwarteng, E. (2005). *African studies in a Canadian academy: A tool for liberation or marginalization?* OISE/University of Toronto.

Freire, P. (1996). *Pedagogy of the oppressed.* The Continuum International Publishing Group.

Freire, P. (1970). *Pedagogy of the oppressed* (Trans.). Continuum.

Freire, P. (1997). *Education for a critical consciousness.* Seabury.

Freire, P. (1997). *Pedagogy of freedom. Ethics, democracy, and civic courage.* Rowman & Littlefield Publishers Incorporated.

Freire, P. (2005). *Teachers as cultural workers.* Westview Press

Garibaldi, A. (1986). Sustaining Black educational progress: Challenges for the 1990s. *The Journal of Negro Education*, (55), 386–396.

Giroux, H. A. (2004). Critical pedagogy and the postmodern/modern divide. *Teacher Education Quarterly*, 31–46.

Gonzales, N., Moll, L., & Amanti, C. (2005). *Funds of knowledge*. Lawrence Erlbaum Associates.

Hale-Benson, J. (1986). *Black children: Their roots, culture, and learning styles*. Johns Hopkins University Press

Hall, H. (2009). Tensions, ironies, and social justice in Black civil rights. Lessons from Brown and King. In. W. Ayers, T. Quinn, & D. Stovall, *The handbook of social justice in education* (pp. 43–50). Routledge.

Hancock, D. R., & Algozzine, B. (2006).*Doing case study research. A practical guide for beginning researchers*. Teachers College Press.

Hardwood, S., Browne Huntt, M., Mendenhall, R., & Lewis, J. A. (2010). *Racial microaggressions at the University of Illinois at Urbana-Champaign: Voices of Students of Color living in university housing*. Urbana, Center on Democracy in Multicultural Society. University of Illinois.

Harper, S. (2004). Gender differences in students engagement among African American Undergraduates at historically Black colleges and universities. *Journal of College Student Development, 3*(45), 271–284.

Hechter, M. (1975). *International colonialism*. University of California Press.

Herstein, R. J., & Murray, C. (1996). *The bell curve. Intelligence and class structure in America life*. Free Press Paperbacks.

Hernandez, H., (2000). *Multicultural education: A teacher's guide to linking context, process, and content* (2nd ed.). Prentice-Hall.

Hernandez, D., & Rehman, B. (2002). *Colonize this! Young women of color on today's feminism*. Seal Press.

Holland, D., Lachicotte, W., Skinner, D., & Cain, C. (1998). *Identity and agency in cultural worlds*. Harvard University Press.

Hooks, B. (1981). *Ain't I a woman: Black women and feminism*. South End Press.

Hooks, B. (1989). *Talking back: Thinking feminist, thinking Black*. South End Press.

Hooks, B. (1994). *Teaching to transgress. Education as the practice of freedom*. Routledge.

Hooks, B., & West, C. (1991). *Breaking bread: Insurgent Black intellectual life.*South End Press.

Horton, M., & Freire, P. (1990).*We make the road by walking. Conversations on education and social change*. Temple University Press.

Hurtado, S., Milem, J. F., Clayton-Pedersen, A. R., & Allen, W. R. (1999). Enacting diverse learning environments: Improving the climate for racial/ethnic diversity in higher education (ERIC Document Reproduction Service No. ED430514).

ASHE-ERIC Higher Education Report, 26. Office of Educational Research and Improvement.

Institutional Research Planning and Outome Assessment. (2010). *College of the Southwest campus six-year graduation rates of NM lottery scholarship recipients by ethnicity for first-time, full-time, degree-seeking undergraduate students fall co-horts 2000 through 2003 2000-.* Southwest Region.

Irwin, R., & Pinar, W. F. (2005). *Curriculum in a new key: The collected works of Ted Aoki.* Lawrence Erlbaum Associates.

Irvine, J. (1990). *Black students and school failure: Policies, practices, and prescriptions.* Greenwood Press.

Janesick, V. (2000). The choreography of qualitative research design. Minuets, improvisations, and crystallization. In N. K. Denzin & Y. S. Lincoln, *Handbook of qualitative research* (pp. 379–398). Sage.

Jost, M., Whitfield, E. L., & Jost, M. J. (2005). When the rules are fair, but the game isn't. *Multicultural Education.* Caddo Gap Press.

Kantrowitz, M. (2011). *The distribution of grants and scholarships by race.* Student Aid Policy Analysis Report.

Keller, S. (1988). The American dream of community: An unfinished agenda. *Sociological Forum*, 167–183.

King, J. (1991). Dysconscious racism: Ideology, identity, and the miseducation of teachers. *Journal of Negro Education, 60*, 133–146.

Kincheloe, J. (2004). *Critical pedagogy primer.* Peter Lang.

Kincheloe, J. (2008). *Knowledge and critical pedagogy: An introduction.* Springer.

Kirsch. (2006). Black student college graduation rates remain low, but modest progress begins to show. *Journal of Blacks in Higher Education.* Retrieved from http://www.jbhe.com/features/50_blackstudent_gradrates.html

Kosik, K. (1976). Dialectics of the concrete. *Boston Studies in the Philosophy of Science, 52*, 93–132.

Knapp, L. G., Kelly-Reid, J. E., & Ginder, S. A. (2010). *Enrollment in postsecondary institutions, fall 2008; graduation rates, 2002 and 2005 cohorts; and financial statistics, fiscal year 2008.* National Centerfor Education Statistics.

Knowles, L. L., & Prewitt, K. (1969).*Institutional racism in America.* Prentice-Hall.

Kumashiro, K. K. (2008). *The seduction of common sense. How the right has framed the debate on America's schools.* Teachers College Press.

Ladson-Billings, G. (1995). Towards theory and culturally relevant pedagogy. *American Educational Research Journal, 32*, 465–491.

Ladson-Billings, G., & Tate, W. (1995).Toward a critical race theory of education. *Teachers College Record, 97*, 47–68.

Ladson-Billings, G. (2000). Racialized discourses and ethnic epistemologies. In N. K.

    Denzin & Y. S. Lincoln, *Handbook of qualitative research* (pp. (257–276). Sage.

Ladson-Billings, G. (2006). From the achievement gap to the education debt:

    Understanding achievement in U.S. schools. *Educational Researcher, 35*(7), 3–

    12.

Ladson-Billings, G. (2009). *The dream keepers. Successful teachers of African*

    American children (2nd ed.). Jossey-Bass.

Lorde, A. (1992). Age, race, class, and sex. Women redefining difference. In M.

    Anderson & P.H. Collins (Eds.), *Race, class, and gender: An anthology* (pp.

    495–502). Wadsworth.

Luttrell, W. (2009).The promise of qualitative research in education. In *Qualitative*

    educational research: Readings in reflexive methodology and transformative

    practice (pp. 1–17). Routledge.

Luttrell, W. (2009). Interactive and reflexive models of qualitative research design. In

    W. Lutrell, *Qualitative educational research: Readings in reflexive methodology*

    and transformative practice (pp. 159–163). Routledge.

Lynch, R. V. (2002). *Mentoring across race: Critical case studies of African American*

    students in a predominantly White institution of higher education. Presented at

    the Annual Meeting of the Association for the Study of Higher Education.

    Sacramento, CA.

Marable, M. (1998). *Black Leadership: Four great American leaders and the struggle for civil rights.* Columbia University Press.

Marable, M. (2006). *Living Black history: How reimagining the African American past can remake America's racial future.* Basic Books.

Marcuse, H., (1972). *Counterrevolution and revolt.* Beacon Press.

Marshall, C. (1991). Educational policy dilemmas. In K. Borman, P. Swami, & L. Wagstaff, *Contemporary issues in education* (pp. 1–21). Ablex.

Marshall, C. (1997). Dismantiling and reconstructing policy analysis. In C. Marshall, *Feminist critical policy analysis: A perspective from primary and secondary schooling* (pp. 1–34). Falmer Press.

Marshall, C., & Rossman, G. B. (2010).The what of the study: Building the conceptual framework. In *Designing qualitative research* (pp. 55–88). Sage.

Marshall, C., & Rossman, G. (2011). *Designing qualitative research.* Sage.

Masursky, D. (1997). *Attrition of low income, first generation, African American students at a predominantly White urban university.* Retrieved from http://www.eric.ed.gov/PDFS/ED461324.pdf

Matsuda, M. J., Lawrence, C.R., Delgado, R., & Crenshaw, K. W. (1993).*Words that wound.* Westview Press.

McLaren, P. (2000). *Che Guevera, Paulo Freire, and the pedagogy of revolution.* Rowman& Littlefield.

McWhorter, J. (2000). *Losing the race: Self-sabotage in Black America*. The Free Press.

Merriam, S. B. (1998). *Qualitative research and case study applications in education*. Jossey-Bass Publishers.

Mickelson, R. A., & Smith, S. S. (2004). Can education eliminate race, class, and gender inequality. In M. L. Andersen & P. H. Collins, *Race, class, and gender. An anthology* (pp. 361–370). Wadsworth/Thomson.

Middlehurst, R. (2008). Not enough science or not enough learning? Exploring the Gaps between leadership theory and practice. *Higher Education Quarterly*, *4*(62), 332–339. Blackwell Publishing.

Miles, M. B., & Huberman, A. M. (1994).*Qualitative data analysis*. Sage.

Mills, C. (1997). *The racial contract*. Cornell University Press.

Mills, C. W. (2010). On intellectual craftsmanship. In W. Luttrell (Ed.), *Qualitative educational research: Readings in reflexive methodology and transformative practice* (pp. 139–145). Routledge.

Mishler, E. G. (2010).Validation in inquiry-guided research: The role of exemplars in narrative studies. In *Qualitative educational research: Readings in reflexive methodology and transformative practice* (pp.288–312). Routledge.

Moore, R. (2004). Racist stereotyping in the English language. In M. L. Andersen & P. H. Collins, *Race class and gender* (5th ed., pp. 410–418). Wadsworth/Thomson Learning.

265

National Centerfor Educational Statistics (NCES). (1990). *The condition of education.* National Centerfor Educational Statistics.

NCES. (2000). *The condition of education.* National Centerfor Educational Statistics.

NCES. (2010). *Student effort and educational progress. Postsecondary persistance and progress.* National Centerfor Educational Statistics.

Oesterreich, H. (2007). From "crisis" to "activist": The everyday freedom legacy of Black feminisms. In *Race ethnicity and education* (pp. 1–20). Routledge.

Ollman, B. (1998). Why dialects? Why now? *Science and Society, 72*(3), 338–357.

Opotow, S., Gerson, J., & Woodside, S. (2005). From moral exclusion to moral inclusion: Theory for teaching practice. *Theory Into Practice,* 303–318.

Parker, L. (1998). Race is….race ain't: An exploration of the utility of critical race theory in Qualitative research in education. *International Journal of Qualitative Studies in Education, 11*(1), 43–55.

Patton, M. Q. (1990). *Qualitative evaluation methods* (2nd ed.). Sage.

Pinar, W. F. (1975) (2000).*Curriculum theorizing: The reconceptualists*. McCutchan Publishing Corporation.

Pinar, W. F. (1975). *The method of currere.* Paper presented at the Annual Meeting of American Research Association, Washington, D.C.

Pinar, W. F., & Grumet. (1976). *Toward a poor curriculum.* Kendall/Hunt.

Pinar, W. (1989). A reconceptualization of teacher education. *Journal of Teacher Education*, 9–12.

Pinar, W. F. (1992). Dreamt into existence by others: Curriculum theory and school reform. *Theory Into Practice, 31*(3).

Pinar, W. F. (1994). *Autobiography: Politics, and sexuality: Essays in curriculum theory 1972-1992*. Peter Lang.

Pinar, W. F (2001). *The gender of racial politics and violence in America: Lynching, prison rape and the crisis of masculinity*. Peter Lang.

Pinar, W. F. (2003). *International handbook of curriculum research*. Lawrence Erlbaum.

Pinar, W. F. (2004). *What is curriculum theory?* Lawrence Erlbaum Associates.

Pinar, W. F. (2005). A lingering note. In W. F. Pinar & R. L. Irwin, *Curriculum in a new key* (pp. 1–85). Lawrence Erlbaum.

Pinar, W. F. (2009). The primacy of the particular. In *Leaders in curriculum studies: Intellectual self-portraits*(pp. 143–142). Sense Publishers.

Rigby, K. (2004). Addressing bullying in schools. Theoretical perspectives and their implications. *School Psychology International,* 287–300.

Roach, R. (2006). Seeking out success. *Diverse: Issues in Higher Education, 24*(15), 14–17.

Rosette, A.S, Leonardelli, G. J., & Phillips, K. W. (2008). The White standard: Racial

    bias in leader categorization. *Journal of Applied Psychology, 4*(93), 0021–9010.

Rovai, A. P., Gallien, L. B., & Wighting, M. J. (2005). Cultural and interpersonal factors

    affecting African American academic performance in higher education: A review

    and synthesis of research literature. *The Journal of Negro Education, 74*(4), 359–

    370.

Rowley, S. (2000). Profiles of African American college students' educational utility

    and performance: A cluster analysis. *Journal of Black Psychology, 26*(1), 3–26.

Rubin, L. (2004). Is this a White country or what? In M. L. Andersen & P. H. Collins,

    Race class and gender (5th ed., pp. 410–418). Wadsworth/Thomson Learning.

Russell, J. (1993). Symposium: In your midst: Contributions of women of Color in the

    law: Introduction on being a gorilla in your midst, or, the life of one Black

    woman in the legal academy. *Harvard Civil Rights-Civil Law Review.*

Schwartz, R., & Bower, L. (1997). *Ain't I a woman, too? Tracing the experiences of*

    African American women in graduate programs in education. AERA.

Sleeter, C. E. (1995). An analysis of the critiques of multicultural education. In J. A.

    Banks & C. M. Banks (Eds.), *Handbook of research on multicultural education*

    (pp. 81–94). Macmillan.

Sleeter, C. E. (2001). Preparing teachers for culturally diverse schools. Research and the
overwhelming presence of whiteness. *Journal of Teacher Education, 52*,94–106.
doi:10.1177/0022487101052002002

Sleeter, C. E. (2001). *Culture, difference, and power.* Teachers College Press.

Sleeter, C. E. (2004). Standardizing imperialism. *Rethinking Schools, 19*(1), 26–27.

Sleeter, C. E. (2005). *Un-standardizing curriculum. Multicultural based teaching in the
standards-based classroom.* Teachers College Press.

Sleeter, C. E.,& Grant, C. A. (1991).Textbooks and race, class, gender, and disability. In
M.W. Apple & L. Christian-Smith (Eds.), *Politics of the textbook* (pp. 78–110).
Routledge, Chapman & Hall.

Smith-Maddox, R., &Solórzano, D. G. (2002).Using critical race theory, Paulo Freire's
problem-posing method, and case study research to confront race and racism in
education. *Qualitative Inquiry, 8*(1), 66–84.

Smith, W., Solórzano, D., Ceja, M., &Yosso, T. (2009). Challenging racial battle fatigue
on historically White campuses: A critical race examination of race related
stress. *Harvard Educational Review*, 650–691.

Solórzano, D., Ceja, M., &Yosso, T. (2000).Critical race theory, racial
microaggressions, and campus racial climate: The experiences of African
American college students. *The Journal of Negro Education, 69*, 60–73.

Solórzano, D. G., & Bernal, D. D. (2001).Examining transformational resistance through a critical race and LatCrit theory framework: Chicana and Chicano students in urban context. *Urban Education, 3*, 308–342.

Solórzano, D. G., & Yosso, T. J. (2002). Critical race methodology: Counter-storytelling as an analytical framework for research. *Qualitative Inquiry, 8*(1), 23–44.

Stake, R. E. (1995). *The art of case study research.* Sage Publications.

Stake, R. E. (2000). Case studies. In N. K. Denzin & Y. S. Lincoln, *Handbook of qualitative research* (pp. 555–565). Sage.

Steele, C., & Aronson, J. (1995). Stereotype threat and the intellectual test performance of African Americans. *Journal of Personality and Social Psychology, 60*, 797–811.

Taylor, E., Gillborn, D., & Ladson-Billings, G. (2009).*Foundations of critical race theory.* Routledge.

Terenzini, P., Pascarella, E., & Blimling, G. (1996). Students' out-of-class experiences and their influence on learning and cognitive development: A literature review. *Journal of College Student Development, 37*, 149–162.

Tatum, B. D. (2003). *"Why are all the Black kids sitting together in the cafeteria?" and other conversations about race.* Basic Books.

U. S. Census Bureau. (2011). *Statistical abstract of the United States: Degrees earned by level and sex 1960-2008* [Table 295]. Retrieved from http://www.census.gov/compendia/statab/2011/tables/11s0295.pdf

U. S. Census Bureau. (2011). *Families by type, race, and Hispanic origin* [Table 66]. Retrieved fromhttp://www.census.gov/compendia/statab/2011/tables/11s0066.pdf

U. S. Census Bureau. (2011). *Money income of families--Distribution by family Characteristics and income level: 2008* [Table 697]. Retrieved from http://www.census.gov/compendia/statab/2011/tables/11s0697.pdf

United States Equal Employment Opportunity Commission. (2011). *2010 Job patterns for minorities and women in private industry (EEO-1)2010 EEO-1 National Aggregate Report*. Retrieved from http://www1.eeoc.gov/eeoc/statistics/employment/jobpat-eeo1/2010/index.cfm#select_label

United States Equal Employment Opportunity Commission. (2011). *Color-based charges FY 1997 - FY 2011*. Retrieved fromhttp://www.eeoc.gov/eeoc/statistics/enforcement/color.cfm

U. S. Department of Education. (2011). *National Center for Education Statistics. The condition of education 2011*. Washington, D. C.

U. S. Census Bureau. (2011). *Statistical abstract of the United States: Degrees earned by level and sex 1960-2008* [Table 295].Retrieved from http://www.census.gov/compendia/statab/2011/tables/11s0295.pdf

U. S. Census Bureau. (2011). *Newsroom: Minority links: Education, economics, poverty*. Retrieved fromhttp://www.census.gov/newsroom/minority_links/minority_links.html

Valencia, R. (1997). *The evolution of deficit thinking in educational thought and practice*. Falmer.

Valencia, R. (2010). *Dismantling contemporary deficit thinking. Educational thought and practice*. Routledge.

Valencia, R., & Solórzano, D. (1997). Contemporary deficit thinking (The Stanford Series on Education and Public Policy). In R. Valencia (Ed.), *The evolution of deficit thinking in educational thought and practice* (pp. 160–210).Falmer Press.

Valenzuela, A. (1999). *Subtractive schooling: US-Mexican youth and the politics of caring*. SUNY Press.

Villenas, S. (2009). The colonizer/colonized Chicana ethnographer: Identity, marginalization, and co-optation in the field. In W. Luttrell, *Qualitative educational research: Readings in reflexive methodology and transformative practice* (pp. 345–362). Routledge.

Watson, Z. E. P., Dumas, C. M., Mason, O., Haynes, H., & Dumas, T. (1994). *The relationship between Black student level of academic success and academic advisement: A case study.*

Wellman, D. T. (1977). *Portraits of White racism.* Cambridge University Press.

Wertsch, J. V. (1998). *Mind as action.* Oxford University Press.

West, C. (1993). *Race matters.* Beacon Press.

Why aren't there more blacks graduating from college? (2000–2001). *The Journal of Blacks in Higher Education, 30,* 90–96.

Why Blacks are more likely than Whites to drop out of college. (2002). *The Journal of Blacks in Higher Education, 36,* 51.

Wilds, D. J., & Wilson, R. (1998). *Minorities in higher education.* American Council on Education.

Williams. R. (1966). Prejudice and society. In J. P. Davis (Ed.), *American Negro reference book* (pp. 727–730). Prentice-Hall.

Yin, R. (2003). *Case study research. Applied social research methods series* (Vol. 5). Sage.

Yin, R. (2004). *The case study anthology.* Sage.

Yosso, T. (2005). *Critical race counterstories: Along the Chicana/Chicano educational pipeline.* Routledge.

Yosso, T. (2005).Whose culture has capital? A critical race theory discussion of

community cultural wealth. *Race Ethnicity and Education*, *8*(1), 69–91.

Made in the USA
Monee, IL
07 September 2020